FIVE
STONES

There is no better way to learn and grow than from storytelling and life experiences. *Five Stones* provides both and is a unique blend of biblical and personal stories about giants we all have or will probably confront and how to handle them successfully. A must read written by two outstanding leaders.

Gary Shorb, President and CEO, Methodist Healthcare

Using the age-old story of David and Goliath as a conceptual platform, Brad Martin and Reverend Shane Stanford's uplifting and pragmatic new work, *Five Stones,* reveals a clear, direct, and boldly insightful look into the face of life's difficulties and provides a scripture-based "training guide" to help people from all walks of life take on and vanquish their own "giants" of adversity and struggle.

John Hunter, Inventor of the World Peace Game

Having personally known and been inspired by Shane Stanford for twenty years, I am familiar with some of the giants he has faced in his life and ministry. With keen insights, personal experiences, and spiritual depth, he and Brad Martin have crafted a helpful resource for all of us. Building on basic principles through devotional time and discipline, this book will be a valuable guide for facing and defeating the "giants" of our lives.

Bishop Larry Goodpaster, Former President, UMC Council of Bishops

Brad Martin and Shane Stanford are uniquely gifted and successful men and their insights and personal transparency in writing *Five Stones: Conquering Your Giants* provide a powerful guide that will encourage you, teach you, and lift your spirit—it did mine!

Ken Edmundson, author of *Short Track CEO* and *Listen! You're Trying to Tell You Something,* Chairman Emeritus of The LEDIC Management Group

This is not just a leadership book. Certainly, it is that in an excellent way, but it is also far more. It is a book for everyone who needs help living in the daily grind. This is not theoretical. No abstractions here. The message of the Five Stones has been lived. What a delight it is to receive this powerful guidance from a preacher and a layman! These men walk the talk, and you will feel their heartbeat and passion for vibrant wholeness and life that really matters.

Maxie Dunnam, President Emeritus, Asbury Seminary

SHANE STANFORD
R. BRAD MARTIN

FIVE
STONES

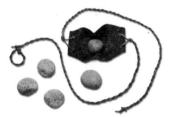

Conquering Your Giants

Abingdon Press
Nashville

FIVE STONES: CONQUERING YOUR GIANTS

ISBN 978-1-4267-7172-9

Library of Congress Cataloging-in-Publication Data has been requested.

13 14 15 16 17 18 19 20 21 22—10 9 8 7 6 5 4 3 2 1
MANUFACTURED IN THE UNITED STATES OF AMERICA

DEDICATION

From Shane

—*For my girls, Pokey, Sarai Grace, Juli Anna and Emma Leigh—who stand with me against the giants (and occasionally stick their tongues out at them too)*

—*For Brad, the dearest of friends, whose partnership for this project taught and meant more than any words on any page*

—*For Jack, a giant killer in his own right, whose example offers a daily glimpse and reminder as to why "the fight" matters far beyond the battlefield*

From Brad

To my wife, Dina, a gift God placed into my picture.

To Jimmy and Dee Haslam, with admiration and appreciation for their inspiration, goodness, and service.

To the remarkable people of L'Arche, who face this life's giants with resolve and gratitude and who claim victory in the next life with great confidence.

And to Henri Nouwen, I hope you have many new books for us to read when we join you in heaven.

Contents

ACKNOWLEDGMENTS

From Shane

It is only through the patience of those who mean so much to me, both personally and professionally, that what we read and share together in these pages came to be. I have no other words but thank you.

As always, and as with every project of which I have had the privilege to be a part, there are those for whom my debt of gratitude is too much to repay (or even figure the exact cost). And yet, they stand by me, cheer me on, and say the right things at the right moment so that what God is pulsing in my heart might land on the page. They are as much (if not more) responsible for what you read as I am. For each of you—thank you!

However, there are those whose specific contributions make a special difference. To Paul Franklyn, Constance Stella, and the team at Abingdon Press, thank you for your continued patience and support. I can't say enough about working for such good, godly people.

To Chip MacGregor, your counsel and support continue to set the boundaries for where the path leads. You are more than an agent; you are a dear and treasured friend.

To my Christ Church family, thank you for making a job more than a job and a church feel like home.

To Scott, Bob, Karen, Emily, your continued support, prayers, and friendship kept the right giant in front of me at the right time—thank you.

To Anthony, your constant "read throughs" and suggestions helped take down more than one giant of uncertainty and confusion.

To Maxie, your guidance and wisdom means more than words.

To Anita, your assistance, patience, and perseverance always keep the truly important matters ahead of the chronically urgent.

To family and friends, thank you for your prayers, care, and support that make the journey seem so part of our daily routine.

To Patty and Nanny, thank you for making me a part of the family, so early on and so completely. "In-law" gave way to "without distinction" years ago. My appreciation is outweighed only by my affection.

To Mom, Buford, Whitney, and Dad, thank you for standing in the gap from the beginning. I love you and I am honored to be a branch on the vine.

To Brad, thank you for making your already very busy life accessible all the more. I could not imagine it was possible to respect and admire you more than I already did—until I wrote a book with you. You are the real deal, my friend, and I am your greatest fan.

To Sarai Grace, Juli Anna, and Emma Leigh. Thank you for running fastest and cheering loudest. I keep swinging against the giants because of you.

To Pokey, thank you for charging against the giants with me. You are the fiercest, sweetest warrior I know. I love you.

To Jesus, as I have said many times—I stand amazed by what you make beautiful. I stand in awe of how you do it.

From Brad

A thorough list of acknowledgements of those who have contributed to the stories I share in *Five Stones* would be longer than the book itself. Furthermore, it is not possible to categorize the effect on my life of these people into discrete areas of impact, as their influence is not confined to some arbitrary bounds. I am simply blessed beyond imagination by many who have inspired, instructed, mentored, supported, forgiven, and loved me.

I am particularly grateful to my family—Bob* and Ann Martin, Brian Martin and Marika Blades, Jeff and Diane Martin, Dan and Micki Martin, Rawleigh and Julie Martin, Myles, Wesley, and Jack Martin, Jack and Mardy Miller, and Jean Kirk.

I am indebted to so many who helped me pursue my opportunities and meet my challenges, including the Haslam family, Dr. Willard R. Sparks,* Frederick W. Smith, Senator Lamar Alexander, Frank Watson Jr., Bobby Cox,* Ronald de Waal, Leroy and Ann Hidinger, Jim and Fran McGlothlin, Henry Loeb,* Edmond Cicala,* Bo Henry, Billy Hyman, Governor Winfield Dunn, Senator Curtis Person Jr., Gerald Tsai,* Ken and Josie Natori, John and Laura Pomerantz, Dudley and Ann Langston, Steve and Karin Sadove, Dr. Harold Beatty,* Dr. Maxie Dunnam, Dr. Bill Bouknight, Carl Nelson, Rev. Stephen Bauman, John and Marion Sue DeFoore, Dr. Scott Morris and Mary

Gilleland Morris, John Kilzer, Jan Averwater, Ron Terry, SL Kopald, Jim Gray, Vernon Brown,* Ray and Ben Jeter Longmire,* Dr. Cecil Humphreys,* Dr. R. Eugene Smith,* Jimmy Lackie, Ron Poe, William Cope Moyers, Dr. Shirley Raines, Robert Carter, the Beall family, Judy Baird, Donnie Fleischhauer, Scott Imorde, Terry Courtenay, Jim Coggin, Doug Coltharp, Donald Wright, Julia Bentley, Eric Faires, Cole Piper, Terry Lethco, Phyllis Moyers, and Barbara Hall.

And I have the deepest appreciation for those with whom I have worked during my experiences with Proffitt's, Saks, RBM, Pilot/Flying J, FedEx, First Horizon, Dillard's, Chesapeake, Harrah's, Gaylord, Ruby Tuesday, lululemon athletica, Custom Foods, Stellar, and the University of Memphis.

My thanks to Shane Stanford for spending this special time with me and insisting I use my voice for the project. And to Abingdon Press for realizing that regardless of one's training or background, we can learn from each other how to confront giants and do so empowered by the strength that can only come from God.

*Deceased.

THE STORY OF DAVID AND GOLIATH

(COMMON ENGLISH BIBLE)

1 Samuel 17:20-54

So David got up early in the morning, left someone in charge of the flock, and loaded up and left, just as his father Jesse had instructed him. He reached the camp right when the army was taking up their battle formations and shouting the war cry. Israel and the Philistines took up their battle formations opposite each other. David left his things with an attendant and ran to the front line. When he arrived, he asked how his brothers were doing. Right when David was speaking with them, Goliath, the Philistine champion from Gath, came forward from the Philistine ranks and said the same things he had said before. David listened. When the Israelites saw Goliath, every one of them ran away terrified of him. (Now the Israelite soldiers had been saying to each other: "Do you see this man who keeps coming out? How he comes to insult Israel? The king will reward with great riches whoever kills that man. The king will give his own daughter to him and make his household exempt from taxes in Israel.")

David asked the soldiers standing by him, "What will be done for the person who kills that Philistine over there and removes this insult from Israel? Who is that uncircumcised Philistine, anyway, that he can get away with insulting the army of the living God?"

Then the troops repeated to him what they had been saying. "So that's what will be done for the man who kills him," they said.

When David's oldest brother Eliab heard him talking to the soldiers, he got very mad at David. "Why did you come down here?" he said. "Who is watching those few sheep for you in the wilderness? I know how arrogant you are and your devious plan: you came down just to see the battle!"

"What did I do wrong this time?" David replied. "It was just a question!"

So David turned to someone else and asked the same thing, and the people said the same thing in reply. The things David had said were overheard and reported to Saul, who sent for him.

"Don't let anyone lose courage because of this Philistine!" David told Saul. "I, your servant, will go out and fight him!"

"You can't go out and fight this Philistine," Saul answered David. "You are still a boy. But he's been a warrior since he was a boy!"

"Your servant has kept his father's sheep," David replied to Saul, "and if ever a lion or a bear came and carried off one of the flock, I would go after it, strike it, and rescue the animal from its mouth. If it turned on me, I would grab it at its jaw, strike it, and kill it. Your servant has fought both lions and bears. This uncircumcised Philistine will be just like one of them because he has insulted the army of the living God.

"The LORD," David added, "who rescued me from the power of both lions and bears, will rescue me from the power of this Philistine."

"Go!" Saul replied to David. "And may the LORD be with you!"

Then Saul dressed David in his own gear, putting a coat of armor on him and a bronze helmet on his head. David strapped his sword on over the armor, but he couldn't walk around well because he'd never tried it before. "I can't walk in this," David told Saul, "because I've never tried it before." So he took them off. He then grabbed his staff and chose five smooth stones from the streambed. He put them in the pocket of his shepherd's bag and with sling in hand went out to the Philistine.

The Philistine got closer and closer to David, and his shield-bearer was in front of him. When the Philistine looked David over, he sneered at David because he was just a boy; reddish brown and good-looking.

The Philistine asked David, "Am I some sort of dog that you come at me with sticks?" And he cursed David by his gods. "Come here," he said to David, "and I'll feed your flesh to the wild birds and the wild animals!"

But David told the Philistine, "You are coming against me with sword, spear, and scimitar, but I come against you in the name of the LORD of heavenly forces, the God of Israel's army, the one you've insulted. Today the LORD will hand you over to me. I will strike you down and cut off your head! Today I will feed your dead body and the dead bodies of the entire Philistine camp to the wild birds and the wild animals. Then the whole world will know that there is a God on Israel's side. And all those gathered here will know that the LORD doesn't save by means of sword and spear. The LORD owns this war, and he will hand all of you over to us."

The Philistine got up and moved closer to attack David, and David ran quickly to the front line to face him. David put his hand in his bag and took out a stone. He slung it, and it hit the Philistine on his forehead. The stone penetrated his forehead, and he fell facedown on the ground. And that's how David triumphed over the Philistine with just a sling and a stone, striking the Philistine down and killing him—and David didn't even have a sword! Then David ran and stood over the Philistine. He grabbed the Philistine's sword, drew it from its sheath, and finished him off. Then David cut off the Philistine's head with the sword.

When the Philistines saw that their hero was dead, they fled. The soldiers from Israel and Judah jumped up with a shout and chased the Philistines all the way to Gath and the gates of Ekron. The dead Philistines were littered along the Shaarim road all the way to Gath and Ekron. When the Israelites came back from chasing the Philistines, they plundered their camp. David took the head of the Philistine and brought it to Jerusalem, but he put the Philistine's weapons in his own tent.

A Shepherd Boy
and a Giant
Killer

by Shane Stanford

"There are two kinds of people—those who think they can and those who think they can't...and they both are right."
– Henry Ford

My name is Shane Stanford, and I am a giant killer. I'm not talking about the giants of fables and lore, but the real kind, the ones that keep us up at night and shout at us across the valleys of life. You know the ones I'm describing. All of us, at one moment or another, have been called out by a giant who stormed into our path, demanding a fight. One friend battles the giant of cancer; another friend battles the giant of addiction. A single mother battles the giant of a wayward teenage son. A faithful employee battles the giant of dishonesty and deception among colleagues at the office. So many battle the giants of insecurity and instability.... I'm sure you can finish this list with the names of giants that plague you and your loved ones. Giants are not new to the human experience; we have just forgotten how to talk about them—and, greater still, we've forgotten how to defeat them.

My first real battle with a giant happened when I was just sixteen years old. By battle, I am talking about the taunting, fear, rage, and, finally, the hand-to-hand combat that I experienced, which felt like life and death were in the balance.

It was during the summer of 1986, and I went to bed with the world on a string. I was captain of the golf team, president of my student class, and dating the prettiest girl in school. That same summer, my doctor told me that I was also HIV positive, contracted from medicines (made of human blood donations) used to treat my hemophilia. At the time, there were no medicines or "cocktail" regimens available to patients with HIV, only the sobering reality of a life that would most likely end in suffering. As you can imagine, my world collapsed. The giant of despair grabbed me and beat me without much resistance.

My grandfather was always my trusted mentor, the one person I knew I could count on no matter what the circumstances. We had a routine of sharing every other Sunday morning together, sitting on the edge of a slope overlooking some family property. The view was not much to brag about; but when I was there with my grandfather, it felt as though we had summited Mt. Everest. Everything just seemed possible in his presence.

A few weeks after my diagnosis, my grandfather could tell that I was struggling with what it meant for my future. As we sat on the side of the hill one cool morning, he asked me, "What are you going to do with this thing?" I knew exactly what the thing was. He didn't have to spell it out. We all knew that we had a giant on our hands, and it would be difficult—perhaps impossible—to beat it.

My response was honest, though defeated. "I don't think I have any options. It's too big. I don't have any choice as to what I can do."

My grandfather sat for a moment and allowed the words to float away until it was just him looking into my eyes. "Son, you have a tough road ahead of you. This is a terrible situation, and you have every right to run and hide." I remember at this point, my grandfather reached over and grabbed my forearm, almost as an act of solidarity. Then he continued, "But, son, you always have a choice no matter how difficult the situation looks. Sure, you can run and hide. Or, you can stand and fight."

I looked and tears had formed in his eyes. With clinched teeth and mustering as much composure as he could, he finished, "And I believe you will make each day...matter."

For the next few months, my life was one encounter with giants after another. It was as if God sent me every illustration of how our struggles are not meant to be the end of us.

During this period, I heard a sermon on the biblical story of David and Goliath. Of course, I had heard the story many times before, but this particular take on the familiar passage shed a new light on the children's version to which I was formerly accustomed. There were several stark differences:

First, it was graphic. I had no idea that David cut off Goliath's head at the end of the story.

Second, it was personal. You could feel Goliath's rage and hatred, not just at David but also at everyone and everything. But, you also could feel David's determination to defeat the giant.

Third, it was profound. I finally understood that this was not just the end of the fight with the Philistines, this was the beginning of something new as well—namely the start of a new attitude for the Jews that said, if the shepherd boy can do it....

And, finally, it was familiar. I knew what it was like to face a giant who screamed at me and belittled my faith. I knew what it was like to have the world around you say, there really isn't anything else we can do.

I listened to this sermon and heard this story as though for the first time. But, this time I wasn't another person sitting in a pew. I was there, on the battlefield, feeling just as fed up with Goliath's taunts and slander as David was.

Won't anyone do something about this blasphemer? Scripture tells us David asked this question time and again of his brothers and friends in the Judean army, but the army remained on the sidelines. "Okay," he concluded. "Then I will."

The story of David and Goliath is more than a children's Bible story about slingshots, stones, and giants. It is about being fed up with the voice that is screaming from across the valley.

You can't hear this teaching without hearing what David accomplished. Giants are not just mythical figures in long-ago stories. No, they exist now and still have one overarching goal—to destroy.

My conversation with my grandfather was more than twenty-five years ago. Since that time, I have lived a truly blessed life. I married my high school sweetheart—that "prettiest girl in school," and we have three beautiful daughters. I pastor an amazing church and have achieved successes in my personal and professional life that could only be called miraculous. Pausing at this point in my bio, many would think that I had lived an easy life. But I have faced giants during every one of these twenty-five-plus years—the giant of disease and a broken body; the giant of broken relationships; the giant of despair and confusion; the giant of hopelessness; and the giant of disillusionment—just to name a few. Sure, at times, the fight was graphic, personal, and, certainly, profound. But, the miracle of overcoming these giants was born from the mayhem of each serious challenge and obstacle. Like David, some of the giants I faced throughout the years looked unbeatable, or at the very least, the outcome felt uncertain. And, also like David, at times I heard the whispers of others saying, he is just a shepherd boy. But then I would remember this: in *our* faith, shepherd boys are also giant killers.

The Moment of Decision

As one reads the story of David and Goliath, the turning point in the story is when David decides to confront Goliath. It is not a coincidence that this encounter happened so early in David's life. Had David the king or warrior confronted the Philistine, it still would have been news, but not the kind of news as when David the shepherd boy showed up. David was a nobody and a frail nobody at that. He was in camp to bring supplies to his brothers, not to be involved in the fight. But David heard how Goliath talked to God's people, and, more important, about God in particular. Thus, David asked, "Will no one do something about this?" And when no response came, David took matters into his own hands.

David was capable of defeating the giant. He just needed a chance. And maybe you just need a chance too. Maybe your giant is difficulty in your marriage, strained relationships with your children, or a broken friendship. Or maybe you confront giants at work, as you manage your organization through a crisis or provide opportunities to move your company to the next level of success. Your giants may be financial problems or health struggles. Maybe your giant is about you, your relationship with God, or the call to do something that seems uncomfortable to you. Whatever your giant may be, it stands between you and what you were meant to be, and you must make a decision as to whether or not you will confront it.

The first critical stages of any battle take place well before you confront the giant, far from the tents of your brothers and sisters and the valley over which the giant calls your name. The first skirmish happens inside you. Sure, you can cower behind the drapes of your tent. Or you can say, enough is enough.

And so, true to form, when I was appointed several years ago as pastor of Christ Church in Memphis, Tennessee—a large, well-respected congregation known for its innovation and leadership—one of the first sermons I shared was the story of David and Goliath. By this time, it was a familiar sermon to those who knew me, part of the standard series whereby my congregation could know more about my teaching and beliefs. Certainly, central to my deepest-held principles is the conviction that our giants—in whatever way they manifest themselves—do not have permission to control our future.

The sermon sparked a conversation with a member of the congregation who would soon become one of my dearest friends and most trusted mentors—Brad Martin. When I arrived at Christ Church, I asked some of the congregation's most experienced leaders who *they* would consult for guidance and wisdom about leading such a large and complex organization of nearly six thousand members. Brad Martin was at the top of that list.

When we met, I was struck by Brad's humility and grace, and I soon came to treasure his wise counsel. I knew of Brad's journey as a businessperson and of his charitable nature, but I had no idea that he had faced his own share of giants as well. Our discussions around the story of David and Goliath became a meeting place for us, and we realized that no matter what form all our giants take, they look and act much the same.

Five Stones is the unfolding of those conversations. What began as private discussions about David and Goliath quickly transitioned into a framework for how any person in any circumstance can face life's giants. During one of our most important conversations, we discussed the ongoing challenges and obstacles that often stop an organization or a person from reaching their full potential. We concluded that difficulties arrive in various forms and attack people from all walks of life. But there was more to these conversations about giants. We realized that, as different as the circumstances could be in how these attacks took shape, there were also common denominators. We discovered four consistent truths:

1. Giants arrive *at any time.*

2. Giants are *not* to be taken lightly.

3. Each giant has strengths *and* weaknesses.

4. Every giant *can* be defeated.

Using this Book

Here's our hope for this book. First, this book is a storybook. At its heart is the story of David and Goliath, but it includes our stories as well. As you continue, we hope you will learn about the stories that have shaped our own journeys and then be willing to share your story with others.

Second, this book is a teaching manual. We believe the principles shared in the individual *Five Stones* chapters are simple and straightforward. We have seen them work with success, and we hope you use these same stones to face the giants in your life.

Third, this is a devotional book. Within the words of the stories and lessons rests a strand of God's Word that we hope will mean as much to you as it has to us. We want you to know how much God loves you, and that this truth will equip you for whatever giants you encounter.

Fourth, this book is personal. Simply put, you were not born to be abused by a giant, and we want to show you how to live like it.

Principles

Just as David used the stones to face Goliath, we believe there are five principles for facing all giants. These five principles are the individual Five Stones that are discussed by chapter in the book. They include: A Picture, Your Tools, A Plan, Your Training, and Your Nerve. It is our hope that you, the reader, will gather these stones and the principles they represent for your journey as you overcome the giants in your own life. Along with these lessons and our belief that your giants do not have to dominate your journey, this book also unveils how we (the authors) used each of these Five Stones and faced giants of our own.

The Training Manual

There is only one way to become a successful warrior against the giants of life, and that is to train. When reading the story of David and Goliath, it is clear that, though this might have been his first battle against a giant, this was not David's first fight. The Training Manual is a spiritual boot camp that focuses on shaping not only your mind but also your heart and soul. The Training Manual includes daily Scripture references, prayers, questions, and exercises that can be read over a course of five weeks to align your heart with God's.

Finding God in the Fight

We know the process of slaying giants may feel overwhelming or unsettling. We have been there. God does not want us to turn away or think we can do this on our own. God's sadness deepens when we believe our story is too screwed up, too scary, or too impossible to save. Why does this sadden God? Because God became like us and took on a story as well, to show us that there is a reason to keep fighting—there is something to hope for and something to learn.

Before Jesus, the people of God understood life from only one angle: God was up there (in the sky, in the fire, on a mountain, in the Temple), and they were down here.

Jesus' death at Calvary changed that. God fought hand-to-hand combat with the giant of death and won. During that fight, the story got personal for God. Just take a look at Jesus' last words on the cross:

Father, forgive them. (Luke 23:34)

Why have you left me? (Matt. 27:46)

Take care of my mother. (John 19:26-27)

I am thirsty. (John 19:28)

It is finished. (John 19:30)

Do those prayers sound familiar to you? They do to me. In one form or another, I have prayed them too. Haven't you?

Reading these words of Christ reminds me that Jesus knows what it is like to be hurt, exhausted, frustrated, forgotten, and concerned about loved ones. Christ knows what it is like to face life's most destructive and painful giants. And, if Jesus knows all of these things, then God also knows. He knows what it is like to wonder if the whole journey is worth it. He knows what it is like to lose a loved one or be betrayed and forgotten. God knows what it is like to say the same thing over and over again and feel as if no one is listening. And, of course, God knows you and understands your battles. That is your new beginning.

Certainly, we don't know specifically where life has led you at this moment, but we know that God has something amazing in store for you. God desperately wants no life to feel it is beyond restoring, or that it does not possess the possibility of redemption. You just have to begin. This book can help you get started.

Over the next chapters, we will help you select five stones—stones you can carry with you into battle against the giants you face. And we will show you how to use these stones with confidence in your ultimate victory.

So, what do you say? Shall we confront some giants?

WAR STORIES

*"We did not all come over on the same ship, but
we are all in the same boat."*
—*Bernard Baruch*

Remembering
(Shane Stanford)

One of my great uncles landed at Normandy as part of the June 1944 D-day invasion. He rarely spoke of the event, except to answer a specific question or two at family gatherings. When my great uncle did answer, his responses were always short, to the point, and he never allowed follow-up questions.

Of course, those of us in the family were fascinated that one of our own had taken part in such an important event in history. Our inquiries stemmed from our adoration of him, but my uncle never wanted to open up. I realized later that whatever happened in those few days on that beach in France was almost more than my uncle could bear to live through, much less rehash time and again over the years.

But we persisted, and I can't remember a single family event that someone did not ask him about the war. Finally, my aunt (his wife) told him, "Just talk to them. They want to know because they care."

My uncle responded sternly, "I don't want to walk down that road again."

"Yes," she said, "But, how will they ever know what you went through?"

"They only need to know one thing," my uncle responded. "We won the fight."

"But, shouldn't they also know *why* you fought at all?" My aunt grinned slightly and then finished, "After all, if they don't remember that, does it really matter that you landed on that beach?"

Remembering is an important concept for any generation. Those who fought in World War II told their stories for many reasons—to recount heroism and warn of tyranny but also to prepare the next generation for the battles to come. Some were personal stories about intimate connections and circumstances that affected a single life, possibly two. Other stories were about entire companies of men whose lives, and the lives of all connected to them, changed in an instant.

This chapter is about remembering. The Christian community treasures the act of remembering. We tell our stories over and over again, as a means of shaping, warning, and encouraging those who will follow. Some stories are about miracles and love. Others tell our heritage as the family of God gathered around his Table. But some stories are war stories, much like my uncle's, and tell when people ran across valleys of fear and doubt and confronted giants in battle.

Certainly, no two giants are exactly alike. One person may encounter the giant of cancer—a deeply personal battle—while another battles global giants, such as pandemic disease, poverty, and despair. Regardless the details, we *remember,* and we value these stories. The stories are valuable not because we may find ourselves in the same situations but because they reveal lessons about the nature of humanity, our ability to overcome obstacles, and the strengths and capabilities that sometimes we forget we possess. Our responsibility is to listen and learn what we can about our fellow human beings, and about ourselves, so that we can apply these lessons to the life that awaits us.

A Child Who Sleeps in Miseri
(Shane Stanford)

Several years ago, a friend of mine left her middle-class life and spent two years as a missionary to Kenya. Many were shocked by my friend's decision. Sure, she had always loved working with church groups and social organizations at various mission locations around the world, but no one could have imagined that she would actually leave life as she knew it and serve full-time. Her decision came after one particular trip that changed her forever.

My friend was only supposed to be in Africa for two weeks when she left on this particular trip, organized through a relief agency. My friend had always been drawn to children, and although she and her husband had tried to conceive for some time, they had no children of their own. Yet God kept placing needy children in her path, and she had already made several trips to work in orphanages in Africa. This particular trip was different. On this trip, she would be working in a day orphanage.

When most of us think of an orphanage, we imagine a place where children without family live and attend school. In Kenya, as in other nations in sub-Saharan Africa, needs created by the HIV/AIDS pandemic have placed excessive strain on institutional services, especially those serving children. For this reason, day orphanages, not residential orphanages, provide basic necessities to those little ones who are the most vulnerable and would otherwise have nothing—truly a last resort for the "least of these" among us.

Upon arriving at the day orphanage in Kenya, my friend met a worker carrying a small girl. The child's body was frail and malnourished, but her face shined with the most beautiful smile. Whereas her body revealed every sign of what is most disturbing and troubling about the plight of children in her country, her face revealed a spirit that was anything but hopeless.

As these contrasting images collided in my friend's mind— the grave circumstances and the child's beautiful face—she greeted the young child with the help of an interpreter. My friend learned that the child's father had died just after she was born; her mother died when she was three. Now she lived with an aunt who also was sick and who could not provide much in the way of care. In fact, the child told our friend that *she* cared for her aunt at night, trying to provide her with as much comfort as possible. Like so many in similar circumstances, this child's life was a difficult, troubling existence.

However, every morning the workers arrived in a goat cart and took the little girl to the day orphanage. Here she found not only food and an occasional change of clothes, but also friends and caretakers with whom she could talk and play. Sure, toys were few, meals meager, and clothes secondhand, but this place in the daylight seemed worlds away from her bare home at night, and it provided what previously appeared impossible: glimpses of hope.

Our friend listened intently as the workers described the little girl's daily routine. "We pick her up," they said in their broken English, "and bring her here so that she might find a little food, some clothes, and some schooling. It is not much, but it is more than she has when she returns to Miseri."

"Returns to where?" our friend asked, not sure that she had heard correctly.

"Miseri," the worker replied. "It is the name of her settlement. The word comes from the Swahili for 'Egypt.'"

Our friend realized that although she had not actually heard the English word "misery," it certainly conveyed the proper meaning. "Misery" was more than appropriate to describe the child's life. After all, what hope did she have? She would not enjoy an abundant childhood like the children our friend knew in the States. She most likely would not grow up to finish school, train for a job, or even have a family. No, the chances for her future were those same impossible odds the disease deals everyone in poverty who suffers from it. This realization hit our friend with a powerful force. She had seen poverty before, especially on her previous visits to Africa. But the situation of this child seemed deeper and more tragic. Yet the child had a beautiful, smiling face.

Standing there, our friend was lost in thought. Where was God? Where was hope? What would effectively confront the onslaught of this disease, not only for this child but also for all children? What could possibly fill the void left by such desolation that wrecked not only a child's present but also her future? My friend paused a moment, lost in sorrow. But then, as she looked up, she saw the child's smile and the embrace of the workers, their love and care for this little one. She saw that in spite of obvious struggles, the people in this picture seemed to express *peace and hope,* a sense of *possibility.* Surrounded by so much sorrow and despair, our friend was amazed by this scene. In it, she found the answer to her questions.

The answer was right in front of her, resting in what she had almost missed. Our friend realized that despite the disease and the impossible circumstances facing this child, nothing was set in stone. Why? Because of the acts of these people who loved, touched, and cared like Jesus—who had become Jesus for the child—misery was not all this child would know.

Though my friend was thousands of miles from her home, this scene was not entirely foreign to her. She had been an "emotional orphan" from the age of seven and had fought this giant her entire life. Though she had two living parents, they had abandoned her—one to addiction and one to personal ambition. My friend had spent her life caring for her younger sister, who fought the giant of depression. From one foster home to another, they lived the best they could in their own version of a day orphanage.

My friend traveled halfway around the world before she defeated the giant she had fought her entire life. By holding onto a picture of love for this child in Kenya, my friend experienced the power of love in her own life. The giant that had terrorized her had to go. No matter what the giant had convinced her of regarding the world, he didn't have a say in how her future unfolded. And, as she framed the picture of that Kenyan girl's faith and life in her heart, she realized God never intended for her own address to be *misery*. It's not meant to be yours, either.

Last Words, or Second Chance?
(Brad Martin)

In 1998 while serving as a member of the Board of Trustees of the American Film Institute, I had the opportunity to cast a ballot to select the AFI top 100 Movies of all time. The Orson Welles' classic, *Citizen Kane,* was named the number one film, and my ballot agreed with this ranking decision. But also high on my list was another movie, which did not receive as much attention from my fellow voters. *Hoosiers,* a 1986 film set in Indiana about a small-town basketball team that wins a state championship, was etched in my mind just as strongly as *Citizen Kane.* For sure, the lead character, Charles Foster Kane, accumulates riches beyond imagination and power unrivaled in his time. But this film depicts a tragic life. In the end, Kane possesses nothing of lasting value; and on his deathbed, Kane's last word is "Rosebud," the name of his childhood sled and a reminder of the last time he was happy. No one present at his death even understood the meaning of the word *Rosebud.* Kane lost his lifelong battle against giants.

In *Hoosiers,* Gene Hackman stars as Norman Dale, the new coach of the fictional Hickory, Indiana, high-school basketball team. Before arriving in Hickory, Dale had been fired from a previous, more prestigious coaching position after hitting a student athlete. He paid the price for losing his battle with the giant, Anger. In the small town of Hickory, Dale sets out to rebuild his life. Also in the film, Dennis Hopper portrays Shooter, the father of a player on the Hickory team and the town drunk. In the midst of extraordinary odds and with very little support, Coach Dale molds the Hickory high-school players into a championship team while challenging Shooter to be his assistant coach, requiring Shooter to confront his giant of addiction. My favorite scene in the movie shows Shooter listening to the radio broadcast of his son's game, cheering from his bed in an alcohol treatment center, as Hickory becomes the unlikely state champion.

Sure, *Hoosiers* is another underdog-versus-favorite story, and we like to see the underdog win. But *Hoosiers* is not just about an underdog basketball team winning a championship game. It is a story of redemption. Coach Norman Dale and Shooter beat the giants that were destroying their lives and their relationships. They won victories far more significant than a state basketball championship.

So which will it be for you? Will you be a Citizen Kane, your last words clinging to something forgotten so long ago that no one comprehends what you are saying? Or will you be a Norman Dale or Shooter and take the first step to build, or rebuild, your life?

It's time to choose.

Two Cathedrals
(Shane Stanford)

Two cathedrals sit opposite each other at the corner of Fifth Avenue and 50th Street in New York City. One cathedral is the Episcopal seat of the Roman Catholic Archbishop of New York; the other is the headquarters for some of capitalism's most fashionable displays.

While St. Patrick's Cathedral and Saks Fifth Avenue point to two different worlds, they stand as neighbors at one of the most prominent real estate locations in the world. Millions of people pass by these cathedrals each year, and untold numbers enter their doors, at Saks perhaps looking for some of the splendor of this life; at St. Patrick's, seeking hope in the life to come.

My co-author, Brad Martin, successfully led Saks Incorporated, the parent of Saks Fifth Avenue, as its CEO for a number of years. Prior to entering the business world, Brad served as a member of the Tennessee House of Representatives. Whether in public service or business activities, Brad believes one's work must have significance and purpose, and he approaches his responsibilities in this manner.

On September 11, 2001, our nation was stunned and our security devastated by terrorist attacks in New York and Washington. In the traumatic and unprecedented days that followed, clergy in the pulpits across our land, from St. Patrick's in New York to my own church in Hattiesburg, Mississippi, rose in their churches to lead congregations and communities to a place of compassion, hope, and resolve. And so did many business leaders such as Brad Martin at Saks.

We used the venue of our churches to proclaim right from wrong. They used the platforms of their commercial enterprises to do the same.

The giant of terrorism did not strike a mere segment of our society. It attacked our very values and our way of life. And so to comfort the hearts and inspire the spirit of our people to *battle,* we joined arms—the faith community and the business community—and resolved that this giant of hatred and terrorism on our land would not stand.

The Stories We Tell

Pearl is a faithful, loving, hard-working wife and mother. Her family is the center of her life, and it doesn't take much time in Pearl's company to grasp this fact and be blessed by it. Pearl's oldest daughter is a delightful child who uses a wheelchair, is legally blind, and faces additional medical challenges. Her bright disposition lightens the load of everyone who crosses her path, and her mother, Pearl, is her primary caretaker.

To watch Pearl and her daughter is to view the most authentic expression of a parent's love. "You would never know that her life is not absolutely perfect," my wife has commented many times. "Pearl makes the world a more joyful place."

Joy. That is the word most used when people talk about Pearl. One day while waiting in the carpool pick-up line at my daughter's school, I noticed a van in front of me and saw Pearl get out of the driver's side. Once she caught sight of her girl, Pearl's face exploded with an amazing smile, the kind you usually see at parties or celebrations. I looked to my right and saw her daughter in her electric wheelchair, approaching. I could not hear the dialog between them, but I didn't need to. Anyone could tell that their reunion was full of happiness and excitement. Their joy was sustained even as Pearl undertook the strenuous task of loading her daughter and the wheelchair into the van.

Since that day, I have gotten to know Pearl and her sweet family better. They are the real deal. They are truly joyful, maybe one of the most joyful families I have ever met. They also fight more giants than most families could ever imagine, as the rigors of caring for a child with disabilities takes a significant physical and mental toll on the caretakers. Providing the best life possible for her daughter, in spite of the struggles and trials, and finding joy in serving and relating to her child is where Pearl claims victory over giants.

Here's what I find most remarkable about Pearl's story: When asked to explain her extraordinary, joyful spirit, she laughs off the question. "Oh, that's crazy," she says. "It's not extraordinary at all. Anyone can have this kind of joy. Because anyone can have Jesus."

Pearl's story matters to you and me, whether we fully realize it or not. I believe God wants us to know the Pearls of this world and her story for more than the tender sentiment it creates in us, because the lessons of her story are more profound than we might first recognize, deeper than the feelings we get from a heartwarming tale. Pearl walks many of the same paths that you and I do, and many that we have not experienced. But Pearl's courage is increased by the fact that she knows she never goes alone. She walks in the constant company of the one who loves us all, more than we can imagine or fully understand. The best way for her to experience this truth is to receive practical and emotional support from those around her—from people like you and me. In that way we join Pearl on the battlefield in her fight against giants. And, we share in her victories.

* * *

David's task began with choosing five smooth stones. There was nothing mystical about this process. David was a shepherd who defended his flock with a slingshot and stones. But David didn't grab just any stones. Scripture tells us that he chose five specific stones for their size and shape. David knew these weapons needed to be the right ones for the task at hand. David was well aware of what a slingshot and a stone could do in the hands of someone skilled to use them—he had fended off animal attacks before. That is why David reminded Goliath, his brothers, and everyone else standing there, "I know this story. Remember, I have fought bears and lions before."

Over the next chapters, we will help you select five stones—stones you can carry with you into battle against the giants you face. And we will show you how to use these stones with confidence in your ultimate victory.

Throughout my own journey, I have paused at the sight of a few giants. Some of my giants, like many of yours, have been enormous and terrifying. I don't have all the answers, and I cannot know what you or I will face at every crossroads. But I do know that I must face the giants standing in front of me now as well as those I will meet in the future. Retreat is not an option. And so, I move forward. As I walk into battle, prepared to engage in the fight, I remember two things: First, I don't fight this battle alone. Second, I am not the first to fight this battle, feel these feelings, have these questions, or need an extra ounce of courage. In such moments I remember the stories of my uncle at Normandy, seemingly washed up coaches, friends who confront their own childhood abandonment by caring for children who have been abandoned, and of a dear, faithful mom who loves her family *through* their struggle.

We share these stories because they contain important lessons. One day you will remember a snippet of a story and the lesson it teaches, and it will be just what you need to face your giant in that moment. And as you journey along in life, you will tell your own stories, and others will remember the lessons of *your* victories.

For now, it is time to prepare for battle.

The First Stone

A Picture

DRAW A CLEAR PICTURE

"A man can't be too careful in his choice of enemies."
— Oscar Wilde

> Your servant has fought both lions and bears. This un-circumcised Philistine will be just like one of them because he has insulted the army of the living God.
>
> —1 Samuel 17:36

A clear picture is critical in battling your giants. The picture must include detail, and it must be as complete as possible. Art scholars teach students that a great picture shows perspective. And Billy Graham declared, "We can see the picture more clearly if we look at it from the cross." That's where we think you should start.

John Beckee was an artist whose career flourished during the 1850s. At first his name was not known beyond the local dealers and artists in the community where he lived, but slowly his reputation grew among the mainstream public. His earliest goal was to be the best artist of his generation. However, Beckee's paintings never received critical acclaim. His themes failed to generate positive response from critics in the artistic world. Yet, Beckee was keenly gifted at sketching out clear pictures of human beings and their actual settings. These pictures were as precise and detailed as a photograph, clearly depicting both the main subject and the surrounding context. Beckee's drawings were so good, many compared them to images created by the new "photo picture machine"—the early camera that made its celebrated debut at this same time.

Beckee's talent was not only exceptional but useful. Law enforcement agencies, in particular, valued his skills. John created renderings of criminals on the loose so that they could be found and brought to justice. He drew pictures of people who were missing or in trouble so that they could be found and given protection.

Some estimate that John Beckee rendered drawings of thousands of people over the course of his career. His work was used to locate missing children, apprehend numerous criminals, and identify persons for various other legal reasons. His work made a difference in people's lives as a catalyst for justice. There is certainly an important and deserved place for fine art in our world. But, at times, a simple, clear picture can be invaluable.

Before law enforcement could begin to investigate a case, they had to start with Beckee's drawing in hand. Likewise, before we can conquer our giants, we must start by picturing the outcome we desire. We must focus on a clear image of what we hope to accomplish and envision where we are going. Surely young David focused on the outcome he desired when he faced his giant. There were many possible outcomes at that moment on the battlefield: The giant could have exploded into a new rage and crushed the shepherd boy. He might have been injured by David's first stone and run back to his camp. Or, he might have changed his mind about the whole thing and simply walked away, leaving David and the Israelites alone. But David did not focus on any of those alternative outcomes. Instead, he envisioned the giant dead, powerless, and lying bloody and lifeless on the ground. We must focus on a clear picture of what we are aiming for and where we are going, but we must also picture how we will get there.

Seeing the Shot

Among the last generation of professional golfers, most agree that Jack Nicklaus was the greatest champion. For the past forty years, two generations of golfers have sought to emulate Nicklaus' example of success both on and off the course.

Nicklaus is a fascinating person. Incredibly well organized, he approaches each facet of his life from a very disciplined perspective. Over the years, this has included everything from his golf swing to his design of a new golf course.

In Nicklaus' classic golf instruction book, *Golf My Way*, Nicklaus shares a significant principle for his success. He calls it "seeing the shot." Nicklaus is a firm believer in the fact that every shot in golf (whether a long shot or a short one) requires one swing. But, one of the most important parts of the shot happens before ever hitting the ball.

Nicklaus would stand behind the ball to begin his pre-shot routine. He would find a point just ahead of the ball that was on the line of his target, and then he would "imagine the shot." That's right, before he ever hit a single golf shot, Nicklaus would envision the shot in his mind, painting a clear picture of how he believed the shot should fly.

Nicklaus believed that by seeing the shot, the mind sent signals to the body during the golf swing (which is basically a series of muscle memory executions) and, thus, assisted the body during the actual shot as though the body had experienced the shot before. This technique became popular with the next generation of golfers, and the pre-shot routine became as important as the swing itself. It gave the golfer a mental picture of what he or she wanted to happen.

But, Nicklaus was not the only great athlete to use this technique. Hall of Fame running back, Jim Brown, used to sit in front of his locker before games and "see" everything that he believed could happen during the game. He would then purposefully (in his mind) remove any negative images and focus only on the positive ones. Brown considered this mental preparation as critical to his success as his actual execution on the field.

Sports psychologists call this technique *visualization*. Visualization is the creation of positive images in the mind before practice and competition—in short, seeing yourself succeed. Its purpose is to simulate the game as clearly and vividly as possible, to create a déjà vu experience when performing in real time. Then, once in the real-time situation, your procedural memory, or muscle memory, is engaged, and your body responds accordingly, almost instinctively. The result increases a reaction time whereby you have programmed the mind and body to perform automatically and without hesitation. Speeding up this reaction time, if only minutely, can be the difference between executing at a high level or coming up short.

In the story of David and Goliath, one of the first tactics we see David use is to distinguish between Goliath the mythical figure and Goliath the champion warrior who could be killed. The rumors that spread throughout the Israelite encampment had Goliath so completely dominating the Israelites' psyche that most of the Israelite soldiers were defeated long before they entered battle.

Sound familiar? Do you often feel defeated before you even begin the battle? How might your life be different if you developed a strong *spiritual* muscle memory? What if your thoughts and actions were consistently moving toward a positive outcome? What would it be like to feel empowered, capable, and confident? We must remove the obstacles of fear and distorted imagery, as they cloud our thinking, dampen our resolve, and drag us into a state of inertia and sometimes even hopelessness. We must replace these obstacles with clear and positive images of our desired outcome.

Finding Clarity

In order to find clarity, draw a clear picture of your desired outcome and visualize how you will get there, developing your spiritual muscle memory so that you think and act instinctively, with positive motion toward your goal. But how, exactly, do you draw a clear picture? Follow these steps to help you clarify your own thoughts and conclusions when you face a challenge, so that your picture will come into focus.

1. Separate fact from fiction.

2. See the complete picture.

3. Set achievable goals.

Separate Fact from Fiction

There is a great story that dates from the Civil War about an encounter between a young Union soldier and Abraham Lincoln. Lincoln, who loved to walk over from the White House to the nearby Willard Hotel in order to calm his mind, arrived at the hotel one afternoon and sat in the front parlor. Across from Lincoln's sofa was a young Union soldier who was newly appointed to the staff of one of the Army's generals. He was waiting on his commander to come down from his room.

Lincoln struck up a conversation with the young soldier about the progress of the war. The young soldier was new to conflict and still wide-eyed about the uniforms, the fanfare, and the glory of it all. After a bit of conversation, Lincoln asked the young man what he thought was the most important reason for the recent successes that the young soldier referenced, and the young man replied, "It is the leadership of President Lincoln, sir." Before Lincoln could offer a word of deference for the compliment, he realized that the young man had no idea who was sitting across from him.

"Tell me about the President," Lincoln asked.

"Oh, he is a giant of a man" the young solider answered. "It is rumored that he walks as though almost on the clouds. His eyes are like fire, and his voice like the booming of trumpets." The young soldier went on and on about his version of Lincoln—grand, glorious, and completely inaccurate.

According to the story, Lincoln smiled, stood, and shook the hand of the young soldier, and playfully said, "Well, then, with that countenance, I wonder why he has not ended this war sooner." Lincoln knew the difference between fact (who he truly was, Lincoln the *man)* and fiction (the towering, mythical figure the young man portrayed him to be). On the carriage ride home, Lincoln reportedly said to his assistant about the young man's assessment, "I'm glad some of us know the difference."

One of the first things David did when confronting Goliath was to *separate fact from fiction.* As large and destructive as Goliath was, he was still a man, and, thus, not invincible. Underneath Goliath's towering frame, his heart beat the same as David's. In spite of Goliath's brawn and bravado, his forehead was as vulnerable to a hurtling stone as any wild dog that might threaten David's sheep.

In our minds, giants grow larger than life. And, if we experience a few setbacks, they just keep growing until they overwhelm us, and we are convinced they are impossible to beat. Sure, Goliath was big and destructive. But David knew that Goliath was made of flesh and blood, and that the battle was already lost if he allowed himself to believe otherwise.

How about you? Do you believe the lies? Does your giant seem too large to defeat? Look at your challenge objectively, and separate fact from fiction.

See the Complete Picture

The Mayo Clinic in Rochester, Minnesota, is one of the world's leading medical institutions. Nearly one million people fly to the clinic every year from across the globe, to take advantage of its world-class medical care. Although there are now Mayo clinics in large metropolitan areas such as Jacksonville, Florida, and Phoenix, Arizona, the first and primary Mayo campus is in the small city of Rochester, population approximately one hundred thousand.

The Mayo Clinic has an impressive history. In the late 1800s, Dr. William Worrall Mayo arrived in Rochester after completing medical school and began practicing medicine in the southern Minnesota town. For the first several years, he had a normal practice, building a network of specialists that he could call when a patient had a particular issue. This was the beginning of what would be called integrative medicine, a process that Dr. Mayo championed and perfected. However, several years into his practice, a tornado nearly destroyed the Rochester community. If it had not been for the St. Mary's convent from Wisconsin, many debate as to whether the city of Rochester would have survived. Certainly, it would not be what it is today. The nuns heard about the disaster and moved their convent to Rochester to assist with the damage.

The Sisters of St. Mary's spent months helping people rebuild and recover, and they developed a particularly close relationship with Dr. Mayo. Together, the doctor and sisters worked for weeks rebuilding the town and tending to the broken bodies and lives of its citizens.

Given the level of doubt about the future of Rochester itself, Dr. Mayo informed one of his nurses that he was planning to leave Rochester in search of a new practice where he could continue to support his family. According to local legend, the Sisters of St. Mary's made him an offer. They would permanently relocate their convent to Rochester and found a new hospital, if Dr. Mayo would continue to operate his clinic in the city.

Dr. Mayo was skeptical and unsure at first. The task, as he would later describe it, seemed too daunting. However, the Sisters of St. Mary's held onto their ambitious vision. Where others, including Dr. Mayo, saw a nearly hopeless situation, the sisters saw possibility. They saw the bigger picture. The sisters encouraged Dr. Mayo to simply show up and see how things would unfold. And, show up he did. Today, the Mayo Clinic is a world-class institution where people from 150 countries and every state of the union receive life-saving treatment.

Of course, after the near catastrophic tornado, meeting the needs of Rochester seemed too much for one person, let alone the idea that one clinic would grow to eventually meet medical needs of individuals all over the world. To confront and conquer our giants requires first putting the pieces of the picture together in the right place at the right time. Together, Dr. Mayo and the Sisters of St. Mary's started at the beginning. For the sisters, and later for the Mayo Clinic, the picture was big; the possibilities were noble but intimidating.

Two points are important here. First, we must look for the bigger picture, the possibilities that are beyond ourselves and our own interests. We must be open to them, even when they intimidate us. Second, we must start at the beginning, one step at a time. We must keep the whole picture in mind, but focus on the first step, then the next, and so on. It is a given that fighting the giants of our life will be overwhelming at some point or another. It would be foolish to deny this fact. But, much like the old proverb of eating the elephant one bite at a time, conquering giants is a methodical process, and requires commitment to see it through. Seeing a clear picture throughout the process ensures your ability to persevere until that picture becomes reality.

Set Achievable Goals
(Shane Stanford)

My wife, Pokey, and I are two very different kinds of air travelers. Pokey doesn't worry about a thing. She arrives at the airport with minutes to spare, but without a single bead of sweat from worry. She glides to the gate, takes her seat on the plane, closes her eyes, and drifts off to sleep for the duration of the trip.

When I fly, on the other hand, I over-analyze every detail of the trip. If the airline recommends we arrive an hour and a half before departure, I arrive two hours early. I follow all the rules, and I am prepared for as many contingencies as possible. So while Pokey settles down in her seat with her eye mask on, ready to drift off to sleep, I perform my own pre-flight pilot check of the plane.

On one particular flight, a guy sat across from me who was just as nervous as I was. He looked over at me and said, "Can you believe that this thing will actually get airborne?" At this point my nerves had gotten the best of me, so I tried to tune him out. Right before take-off is not the best time for me to have the physics of flying explained to me.

The passenger leaned over and repeated his statement. I finally replied, "Well, I was trying not to think about that right now—with us about to lift off and all."

Undeterred, he continued the conversation, saying, "You know, it really is like strapping yourself to a bullet and being fired across the country, isn't it?"

At this point I wanted to take the mask off Pokey and insist that we get off the plane. And, all the while, the man kept talking about the miracle of aerodynamics. He claimed that talking about the facts of flight made him feel more secure. "The more I understand about flying, the more I'm in control."

I couldn't help but give him the most puzzled look. He was sitting across from me, in the middle of the plane, far from the cockpit. He had no more control over the flight than I did.

If you're like me, you like to be in control, or at least you like to maintain the illusion that you are in control. Of course, there are countless things that we cannot control in life. However, if you think and act from the standpoint of a powerless, control-less person, you will never be able to navigate your daily routine, much less conquer, or even face, your giants. With this fact in mind, evaluate your circumstances. If it is reasonable to conclude that your goal is achievable at all, then you must also consider that *you* can achieve it. At some point, I have to trust that the plane I am seated in has successfully flown before, that there is a trained pilot and copilot at the controls, and that we will get off the ground and then eventually land where we are supposed to land. Although I may not have an in-depth knowledge of physics and aerodynamics, I have flown in aircraft many times. Sometimes you have to believe, in spite of what you can't understand, that something is simply achievable and then be the one to achieve it.

See What Is Coming
(Brad Martin)

When assessing an opportunity, dealing with a challenge, or even facing a giant, a clear picture of the outcome one wants to achieve is critical. Whether it's a task you've been assigned, a challenge you wish to undertake or must contend with, or a giant that appears unexpectedly in your life, you must have a clear picture of how you want encounters such as these to turn out. A clear picture doesn't have to be a complicated picture. It can be unconventional and certainly it can be improbable, but complicating the picture can actually limit chances for success. Certainly, "clear" doesn't mean easy. It may very well take a significant amount of time to get clarity on the opportunity or the challenge, but once you've done so, the picture must be straightforward and easy to understand.

Years ago, as a twenty-one-year-old student at Memphis State University, I was invited to deliver the commencement address at the University's graduation ceremony. I had recently been elected as a member of the Tennessee House of Representatives, and I think the novelty of my election while still a student at the University made me a different, if somewhat risky, choice to deliver such a speech. Even though I hadn't yet graduated, I had attended a few commencements. I couldn't recall the content of any commencement speech I had heard, but I did remember each of them as being long-winded. So I pictured a commencement speech that would take less than three minutes to deliver. And trust me, the preparation required to focus the "picture" I wanted to share with the graduates to just three minutes required significant effort. It would have been much easier for me to write a longer speech.

A few days before the graduation ceremony, I was asked to submit a copy of my speech to the University leadership for review. After seeing my speech, the Vice President of Communications from the University called me and said, "This is a terrific start. Please send the rest of your speech." "That is the complete speech," I replied, "and it will last less than three minutes." I'm convinced if the University had had time to get a suitable replacement, they would have found a new commencement speaker. But on graduation day, I drew the picture I wanted to share and delivered the remarks in three minutes, exactly as I had drawn them up, which included these words:

> As we come here today, we realize that the years left in each of our lives are precious few.
>
> Laugh at yourself, cry at yourself. Even more so—stare at yourself.
>
> Know your capacity and weakness.
>
> Feel the vibrancy of your life. Yet dwell not constantly on yourself.
>
> Look to others, laugh with others, cry with others, hurt with others.

Feel the vibrancy of others' lives.

You don't need me to tell you of the responsibility inherent in what you now have.

Don't you ever forget it!

The applause from the audience lasted longer than my speech.

Picturing myself as a member of the Tennessee House of Representatives while I was still a student in college was perhaps a bit presumptuous but crucial if I intended to seriously pursue my passion for public service at that stage of my life. In high school and college, I had developed a growing interest in serving the community, and I thought that holding government office was the best manner in which I might do something significant to help others. Certainly there was nothing else I could contemplate at such a young age that could give me a comparable forum to have an impact beyond my years. So as a political science student at Memphis State University, a participant in the legislative intern program, and president of the student government, I decided to tackle the challenge of getting elected to the Tennessee House of Representatives.

The picture I drew of the task was a bit daunting. I was twenty years old, had no significant work experience, no college degree, no money, and no name recognition. My opponent was a forty-eight-year-old, two-term incumbent with campaign funding and support from other politicians and had a resume that might suggest superior qualifications. The picture wasn't pretty at first glance, but as I separated fact from fiction, other elements of the landscape emerged. A statistical analysis of the district and its historical vote patterns indicated that there was an unconventional vote path by which I might actually win. And the frame included an opponent who, in spite of superior resources, I believed was not as focused on the interests of the public. I thought I should and could defeat him.

So the picture I drew was one where I became a member of the Tennessee House of Representatives, elected by a diverse cross section of support from the community, and one who would have a positive impact on issues and challenges facing my fellow Tennesseans. I was off and running.

When I shared the picture with others, the common feedback I received was that I would gain experience from this campaign, which I would surely lose, and it would help prepare me for a winnable race in the future. And perhaps that picture was more realistic than mine. But if the picture suggested that I *might* not win, that would surely be the outcome. My picture had to reflect victory.

After not taking me seriously for most of the campaign, my opponent panicked during its last three weeks. The race became heated and intense, and I endured name-calling and a barrage of allegations and insults. While responding calmly to these attacks, I maintained an intense focus on executing my strategy and winning the election. And I was appropriately determined to execute that strategy. As we saw with David, tough battles require that.

So on election night, two days after my twenty-first birthday, the picture I had drawn turned out to be the accurate one. I won the election, became the youngest person ever elected to the

Tennessee House of Representatives, served for ten years, and, I think, I was helpful.

Sure, many of my friends and supporters thought my picture was a dream. But, for me, it was a vision.

On election night at the victory celebration, one of my closest friends and most loyal supporters hugged me with joy and shared, "Well, I really didn't see this coming."

"I did," I replied.

Conclusion

When David made his way to the battlefield to fight Goliath, he must have believed that conquering the giant, no matter how big and daunting a task it had been for those before him, was doable. If he didn't have that confidence, he was defeated long before the fight started.

The first stone in our arsenal must be a clear picture of our desired outcome. This picture must be your own. It is important that you see the victory so that it becomes part of your spiritual muscle memory. This reflex propels you forward even when the adrenaline and the difficulties of the battlefield take their toll. Just remember, you have seen the site before; you have watched victory unfold time and again; and you are ready for what comes next. This giant may be big, ugly, and dangerous, but it is still beatable. You will not be denied.

Take heart, today, the battle belongs to you. Remember, you have seen all of this before. To overcome a challenge or to defeat a giant, you have to "get the picture." Look carefully and clearly. Stare at it. Make it your own.

The Second Stone

Your Tools

SHARPEN YOUR TOOLS

> David strapped his sword on over the armor, but he couldn't walk around well because he'd never tried it before. "I can't walk in this," David told Saul, "because I've never tried it before." So he took them off. He then grabbed his staff and chose five smooth stones from the streambed. He put them in the pocket of his shepherd's bag and with sling in hand went out to the Philistine.
> —1 Samuel 17:39-40

God has given you many gifts—tools that can be used in any battle that you might face. They are uniquely yours and customized to fit your life and your battles. Your tools will work effectively *only* if they are honed and ready. To accomplish this, you must recognize that you *are* gifted. You must not believe that your gifts have dissipated, or that they are not useful, or that they never existed at all. None of this is true. You have been equipped with the tools that are necessary to battle the giants in your life. And now you must sharpen the tools you've been given.

What A Healthy Life "Sounds" Like
(Shane Stanford)

The great violinist Nicolò Paganini willed his marvelous violin to Genoa—the city of his birth—but on the condition that the instrument would never be played. It was an unfortunate condition. The wood from which the violin was made is known for a peculiarity: as long as an instrument made from the wood is handled and played, it remains resonant and useful. But if it is set aside or discarded, it begins to decay.

And so today, Paganini's exquisite, mellow-toned violin is now worm-eaten in its case, valueless except as a relic. The moldering instrument is a reminder that a life withdrawn from all service to others loses its meaning. And, when we allow the gifts that we have been given to sit unused, we fail to fulfill the purposes for which we were created, and the tools gifted to us become useless and out of place.

Decay happens in an unused life as much as in an unused violin.

I learned this firsthand from a friend named Tommy who literally arrived on my doorstep. He was thin, sickly, and obviously in distress. Tommy was crushed by regret and the consequences of bad decisions that had happened over a lifetime of trying to fit the wrong gifts into his life. That is not to say he didn't have the gifts needed for an extraordinary journey. On the contrary, Tommy was especially gifted—in music, with words, and at teaching. However, regret led to one too many drinks, and, before long, the alcohol controlled not only his words but also his decisions. By the time people started raising the issue, Tommy was well past the point of no return, and his tools for doing exceptional things sat in the corner, much like Paganini's violin—worm-eaten and forgotten.

By the time Tommy arrived on my doorstep, he had tried just about every remedy possible to either remove the power of his addiction or to forget why he cared. But, nothing seemed to help. And, so, he found himself standing on the doorstep of a stranger, a preacher, desperate to believe in something. *Anything …*

Tommy and I didn't have much in common beyond our diagnoses of HIV. He was opinionated and flamboyant. I was more reserved and reflective. Tommy liked to push at a person's uncomfortable places. I felt uncomfortable knowing those places existed in any of us at all. Something about Tommy seemed unfinished, and I got the feeling that there was something of great value inside him, buried under the surface of his pain, some gift worth discovering. Other people sensed this, too, and I believe that, at his core, Tommy knew it about himself. Tommy's gifts were evident—they had not dissipated or been removed or rendered useless. The problem was not in the gifts, but in their recipient: Tommy was a remarkable example of "operator error."

Indeed, during the year and a half that we met together to talk about life, we discovered the gifts that God had planted inside of Tommy were not lost. They were very much present, just hidden and out of practice. But Tommy—the "real" Tommy—

was there, resting below the surface. We spent one conversation after another unearthing the tools and gifts that God had given him. Many times, we saw immediately how God was going to put that gift to work in rebuilding Tommy's life. Other times, I watched as the emotion of so many missed opportunities and so much wasted time flooded over him. No grief embraces us with the ferocity of a missed chance for peace, love, or happiness.

Tommy kept wiping off the dust of his life, and I watched as God awakened that part of Tommy who knew how to put his gifts in the right order and to good use. What a joy it was to watch Tommy's God-given abilities engage as he experienced a "re-birth" of faith, confidence, and direction. The more Tommy sharpened his gifts, the more he discovered himself.

God wants us to see the opportunities of life, and to meet its challenges, using the gifts God has provided us. Those gifts are meant to be so deeply a part of us that they overflow at both our easiest and most difficult times, when we are confronting both opportunities and challenges. We notice when this does not happen, don't we? We see the stark results in people's lives when opportunities are lost and challenges overwhelm, when God's profound gifts go unused. You have surely seen this in the life of someone you know, or perhaps your own life. There is one thing more powerful, however, and that is when we see that life and its gifts fully employed once again.

Tommy arrived on my doorstep with utterly shattered hopes, but he became whole as his gifts reemerged against one giant after another.

My wife and I hosted a party in honor of Tommy and his first full year of sobriety. I asked him to play and sing some of his favorite music (and mine too). It was wonderful. Some of those in attendance had only known Tommy during the previous couple of years, as he recovered from addiction. But some older friends who had recently come back into his life also attended that night. They were overjoyed and quite emotional at the sight of their old friend who had "come back to life." They saw a healthy person using sharpened, shiny tools for God's glory.

One observer saw the tears in my eyes as I listened to Tommy play a favorite tune. My friend asked, "What are you thinking?"

"I was thinking that this is what a happy life sounds like."

Once David had decided that he would face Goliath on the field of battle and had created a picture of what his desired outcome would be, it was time to begin preparing for the fight itself. At this point, many around him wanted to help. After all, David was now representing the entire nation of Israel. Everyone, from his brothers to the king, offered assistance.

In fact, King Saul insisted that David take the King's personal armor to wear into battle. It was the finest armor for any soldier, crafted by the most highly-skilled experts. But there was a problem. The armor was designed for a king, not a shepherd boy.

As soon as the armor was fitted around David, it became clear that he could not move, much less use this armor for battle. The king thought he was offering David a favor in loaning him his armor. But it could actually have been the equivalent of a death warrant. This shepherd boy would use a slingshot and a stone to fight the giant. God had fitted them perfectly in his hands.

What tools has God given to you? What are you doing to sharpen them?

Your Song

There is a wonderful story told by a young missionary who moved to the outback of Australia to minister to a particular tribe of the Aborigines. The people of this tribe believed that the human experience was intimately connected to the Earth through the five senses. As the young missionary became acquainted with his new friends, he asked them to talk about their lives in relation to the senses. They described the smells of their neighbors' cooking over an open fire and the "first touch" of a new baby being delivered. Both were important parts of their formational narrative as a people and as individuals.

However, the most powerful description of their existence came from sound. The tribe believed that every person was born with a song. Not American Top 40, but the music of creation, whereby the Earth would literally sing because of this new person's existence. Each person of the tribe believed this song connected him or her to the Earth, their families, and the place to which they were born. Thus, the people of this tribe were a singing people; they sang almost nonstop. We might assume that this incessant singing would be an irritation, perhaps even maddening. But the young missionary did not find it so. In fact, he described each song of each person as belonging to the greater melody and harmony of the tribe.

He recounted the experience of sitting around the campfire with his new friends and listening as each person would sing his or her song. At one point, he communicated that he felt envious of them, because he did not have a song. The chief of the tribe pointed to the young missionary's ears in a gesture denoting the act of listening. And then the chief pointed to the young man's heart, signifying that the missionary had not heard his own song because he was listening with the wrong part of his body.

This story serves as a reminder that each of us has been created within the unique image of the Creator. This is the essence of who we are as humans. We must be sure of this; we must recognize the Creator in ourselves. We must pay attention to the ways this God-reflecting essence is manifested in our lives, and we must use it, *live* from it.

Principle One: Decide What Is at Stake

In the fall of 1944, an officer commanding a platoon of American soldiers received a call from headquarters. Over the radio, this captain learned his unit was being ordered to recapture a small French city recently taken by the Nazis. For weeks, French resistance fighters and other favorable locals had risked their lives to gather information about the German fortifications in that city, and they had smuggled this information out to the Allies in the form of a detailed map of the area.

However, it wasn't just a map with the names of major streets and landmarks; it also showed details of the enemy's defensive positions. It was incredibly thorough. The map identified shops and buildings where German soldiers bunked or where a machine-gun nest had been stationed. Block by block, the Frenchmen gave an accounting of the German units and the gun emplacements they manned. For a captain who was already concerned about mounting casualty lists, receiving such information was an answer to prayer. Certainly, the outcome of the war wouldn't depend on this one skirmish, but it would save countless lives of the men charged with retaking the city.

Before the soldiers moved out to take their objective, the Captain gave each man a chance to study the map. And wanting to make sure they read it carefully, he hurriedly gave them a test covering the major landmarks and enemy strongholds. Just before his platoon moved out, the officer graded the test, and with minor exceptions every man earned a perfect score. The men captured the city with little loss of American lives.

Nearly thirty years after this military operation took place, an army researcher decided to base a study on it. The researcher conducted the study in France, using a group of American tourists as substitutes for the World War II platoon of American soldiers. The researcher gave the tourists the same war-era map of the French village. The men and women studied it for several hours, and then were given the same test. Most of the tourists failed. The tourists were capable, intelligent people. It was reasonable to expect that they would score as well on this test as the group of soldiers from thirty years before. But one significant difference between the groups explained the discrepancy: The soldiers were motivated to learn every detail of the map, because their lives and the lives of their brothers-in-arms depended on it. The tourists had nothing to lose but a little time as part of an unusual vacation experience. (Smalley & Trent). The soldiers knew what was at stake. As you face your giants, do you? Are you more like a tourist or a soldier headed to battle?

Principle Two: Take an Inventory
(Brad Martin)

On the morning of September 11, 2001, I was en route to the airport in Memphis to board a plane for Omaha, Nebraska, where I was scheduled to participate in a charity golf outing hosted by the legendary business leader/investor, Warren Buffett. Five minutes from the airport, I received a call from my oldest son with the shocking news of a plane crash at the World Trade Center. I made a U-turn on the highway and returned to my office to gather more facts on the events and to communicate with my colleagues at Saks Fifth Avenue in Manhattan. As the day went on, I was joined by other members of the Saks–New York leadership team. They had been on a plane en route to Texas, and were forced to land in northwest Arkansas. My colleagues had rented a car and made their way to my office in Memphis, where we monitored the unfolding tragedy. We attempted in the midst of this chaotic time to assess the consequences of the attacks on our New York colleagues and their families, as well as to understand the appropriate decisions we had to make for our company. While communication was intermittent with our New York team, its leaders organized a complete evacuation of our offices and store. Once they were assured that each associate had a secure place to go, my colleagues locked the doors of the stately building on Fifth Avenue and began their long walks out of the city to make their way to safety.

Isolated from our colleagues in New York, my thousands of associates across the country and I felt helpless, and we tried to develop our appropriate response to this heinous attack on our nation and our neighbors. On the afternoon of September

11, we instructed every store in our company to close and all employees to vacate the premises and return to their homes. We gathered that night in front of the television at my office and watched President Bush as he explained what had happened and the resolve with which our nation would meet the giant of terrorism on our soil. The president declared that these attacks would not affect the freedom of Americans as they lived their everyday lives. As my colleagues and I listened to the president, we understood that America must be open for business the next day. This was a stake in the ground for us. Our teams at Saks and our other department store businesses quickly reversed course. We organized a conference call with our three hundred store managers across the country late that night. We made this declaration: "All stores in the company except those in the New York area will open for business tomorrow. Any employee who is not comfortable at work or is needed at home is not expected to be there. We do not anticipate a single sales transaction will occur, as shopping at a department store will not be the focus of Americans for many days to come. But our employees, our customers, our neighbors, our communities, and our enemies must understand. We will endure, we will restore, and we will prevail. We will open for business."

On the morning of September 12, as our stores opened across the nation, a small group of Saks employees gathered in the New York store. The streets outside were hung with the gray residue of all that had been obliterated in the attacks. This small team of employees desperately wanted to demonstrate solidarity with their neighbors and all who were suffering the devastation of the tragic events. One associate asked, "How can our Saks

Fifth Avenue store respond? What can we do to communicate some message of hope and unity?"

"While the doors of our store are closed," one of my colleagues replied, "we still have our windows." That was all it took to inspire action. This small band of colleagues, when faced with an unimaginable giant, paused to take stock. They saw clearly all that had been taken away, but they did not dwell on it. Instead, they looked for what remained, what could be repurposed, what could be used in a new way for this new battle. With that simple but clear picture—"the windows!"—this talented and dedicated team of people went about the work of creating a series of stunning displays in the Saks Fifth Avenue storefront windows lining the New York City streets. These remarkable window displays honored the memory of the victims, the heroism of the responders, the resolve of New Yorkers, and the love of our nation and its way of life.

In the wake of the attacks, many Americans sought spiritual comfort and understanding in their houses of worship. In New York, along with so many other New Yorkers, many of my Saks' colleagues and I visited St. Patrick's Cathedral, the long-time icon of Roman Catholicism in the United States and a spiritual beacon for many. Several weeks after the attacks, I hosted Archbishop Cardinal Edward Egan for lunch at the Saks offices next door to St. Patrick's. I told the Cardinal that, like so many others, my Saks colleagues and I took great comfort in the message of hope and ultimate victory proclaimed within the halls of St. Patrick's during those terrible days. And the Archbishop stunned me by replying that as he walked past Saks on a daily basis, *he* took inspiration from the tributes and solidarity displayed in the windows of the department store next door to the cathedral.

On September 13, the Saks Fifth Avenue New York store reopened. Very few guests entered its doors that day. Shopping was simply not on the agenda for most New Yorkers. But late in the morning, an elderly woman came through the front entrance and walked directly to the Accessories Department, where she was greeted by a Saks associate. "I'm here to buy a pair of gloves," the customer declared. "Yes, ma'am," the Saks employee responded. "I'm pleased to show you our assortment of gloves. But first, may I ask, are you doing okay? How are you getting through all of this?"

The woman gathered herself and replied, "It is horrible beyond my imagination, and I cannot express the depth of the sorrow I feel.... But winter is coming, and I need a pair of gloves."

Many people made unimaginable sacrifices in order to respond to the September 11 attack on our country. At Saks, we kept stores open and created display window tributes. These may seem like relatively small efforts. But for our employees, that "Open" sign and those windows were the unique tools within our grasp, which we knew we could use to play our part in this battle. And so the people at Saks fought the giant of terrorism with beautiful windows and open doors. We took an inventory of the tools at hand and, using what we could, offered our neighbors and customers inspiration, consolation, and a sense of hope. And we helped people to get ready for winter.

Principle Three: Share Your Gifts and Your Battles

Several years ago, two students graduated from the Chicago-Kent College of Law. It is one of the most highly respected law schools in the country. Even without the slightest of distractions, graduating from Chicago-Kent is quite the accomplishment. The highest-ranking student in one particular law school class was a blind man named Overton. When he received his honor just before graduation, he insisted that half the credit should go to his friend and fellow law school student, Kaspryzak. Kaspryzak was not as strong a student as Overton, but they were the best of friends Kaspryzak experienced his own struggles, for he was born with no arms. Overton and Kaspryzak met one another in law school when the armless Mr. Kaspryzak had guided the blind Mr. Overton down a flight of stairs. This acquaintance ripened into friendship and a beautiful example of interdependence. Everyone at the law school knew of their friendship, watching the two men balance each other's difficulties. For instance, the blind man (Overton) carried the books that the armless man (Kaspryzak) read aloud in their common study sessions. Individually, they experienced great hardships, but together they made quite a team. Thus, the individual deficiency of each was compensated for by the ability of the other. After their graduation, they practiced law together, establishing a firm that represented people with disabilities.

Many individuals walk this earth under the misguided notion that they do not have any spiritual tools. However, each of us has been given a gift (tool) that, when used correctly, wins the day. Those tools are to be shared, used to meet not just our own needs but the needs of our brothers and sisters. On our own, we are like a blind man trying to hit a target or an armless man trying to hold a spear. But what happens when we learn to work together? Even David asked for help at the beginning. It was only after he found none that he made the fight alone. We confront our giants most effectively when we go out to meet them hand in hand.

Who are the people you count on in this world? Have you asked them for help? And who in your life is facing a giant, needing help? You will have some lonely battles, to be sure. But God encourages God's people to love and care for one another, to do battle together; this is God's design for life. And each of us is equipped with gifts to share.

Exceptional Normal
(Shane Stanford)

My friend Jack is approaching fifty years old. He has made his living as an attorney. He travels across the country consulting with Fortune 500 companies and other organizations. Jack is an accomplished person with varied interests and hobbies.

Jack played golf at a large SEC school and even considered a career on the Tour. Jack was an amazing athlete, undeterred by any challenge or competition.

In addition to his law practice, Jack is also a successful entrepreneur and businessperson. He is a faithful friend and has provided a secure and stable future for his family.

All of Jack's endeavors have happened within the context of significant challenges. Jack has been fighting Type I Diabetes his entire life. Jack's disease ravages the body, affecting nearly every system. Patients like Jack must be diligent every single day to carefully administer medicines, maintain a strict diet, and stay ahead of the disease. Daily life with Type I Diabetes is a daunting challenge and is, for some, an overwhelming burden.

Early on, Jack's parents determined to give him the best chance for a normal life. They raised him to feel loved, strong, and independent. When Jack was old enough, he was enrolled in normal activities along with his healthy friends. He played sports and worked hard at school. Jack's parents taught him to approach life from a positive point of view. They surrounded him with people who had struggles similar to his own, but whose attitudes were positive. Jack's role models demonstrated that in each challenge lies a new possibility for growth, a new chance to succeed. Jack did not feel sorry for himself. His life felt normal. Others, of course, knew that Jack's accomplishments, especially in the context of his disease, were far from normal.

A newspaper even published an article about Jack. After reading the article, a man contacted Jack and asked to meet with him. Jack was excited at the prospect of making a new friend. But his enthusiasm quickly turned to disappointment. The man was bitter about life. He had endured some difficulties, and felt that the world owed him for his trouble. It seemed to Jack that the man had squandered his own potential, focusing instead on his pain, and blaming everyone around him for the dismal outcomes in his life.

The man's struggles included an addiction to prescription drugs. Jack tried to enroll his friend in an AA group, but the man would not faithfully attend the meetings, even when Jack offered to attend with him.

Jack did some research on Alcoholics Anonymous as part of his effort to help this friend. When he read the twelve steps, number four stood out. In the fourth step AA members pledge to have made "a searching and fearless moral inventory of ourselves." It struck Jack that this step alone could save his friend's life. But Jack also knew that we all must make our own choices. Jack stayed long enough that first meeting to hear one of the AA members share these words, "Life *will* seem overwhelming...." Jack knew it to be true.

Fearless means taking on the world "as we find it," even when it seems overwhelming. Jack had learned that lesson; his friend had not. Not all giants are the same, nor are the circumstances of our individual lives. What is normal for you might be exceptional for me. Our task as giant-slayers is to sharpen our tools and be ready for battle.

Your tools, or gifts, are your second stone. Before we move on to the third stone, we want to remind you that sometimes the hardest part of facing giants is simply standing up to face the task. It is easy to become immobilized, to look for assistance or inspiration or motivation from "out there" somewhere. Those things may come, but the choices and actions are yours to make, regardless. You already have what you need, so you must stand up, face the task, and do something.

Be Useful
(Brad Martin)

This essence, your identity as a child of God, uniquely created in the image of God, is the most important of your tools. It is the starting point of all the other particular gifts you have been given. This essence and all your other gifts are meant to be used against your giants. They are your tools, fitted to your specifications. And they are sufficient. So, now that you recognize the tools at hand, how do you sharpen them?

Decide What Is at Stake

Take an Inventory

Share Your Gifts and Your Battles

My friend Gerald Tsai was a pioneer of the mutual fund industry, and renowned for his skills as an investor and financier. Shortly after finishing his college studies, Gerald went to work at a small mutual fund company, which would ultimately become one of the largest investment management firms in the world. On the first day of Gerald's employment, he reported to his desk thirty minutes before the expected start time, and there he waited the entire day for someone to tell him what to do. It didn't happen.

The next day he was back at his post bright and early. Gerald read the business news of the day, telephoned a few acquaintances in the financial services industry, and awaited instructions from a supervisor. It didn't happen. And so it went for the next three days.

At the end of his first week of work, having received no direction whatsoever on what he was to be doing, Gerald asked for a meeting with the CEO. The meeting was granted, and he entered the office of the founder and chief executive. "Sir," Gerald began, "I have just completed my first week of employment with the company and have yet to receive any instructions from my superiors about what I am expected to do. I come to the office, read *The Wall Street Journal,* connect with acquaintances, and then I wait for instructions. They never come. What do you expect of me?"

"Gerald," the CEO replied, "during your interview process, it was very apparent to me that you are a person with many gifts. Your job is to be useful."

You have all the tools and the gifts that you need. Now, be useful.

The Third Stone

A Plan

DEVELOP A PLAN

"Failing to prepare is preparing to fail."
—*John Wooden*

> But David told the Philistine, "You are coming against me with sword, spear, and scimitar, but I come against you in the name of the Lord of heavenly forces, the God of Israel's army, the one you've insulted. Today the Lord will hand you over to me. I will strike you down and cut off your head! Today I will feed your dead body and the dead bodies of the entire Philistine camp to the wild birds and the wild animals. Then the whole world will know that there is a God on Israel's side. And all those gathered here will know that the Lord doesn't save by means of sword and spear. The Lord owns this war, and he will hand all of you over to us."
> —1 Samuel 17:45-47

David's objective was to defeat Goliath and rescue Israel from impending destruction. He had formulated a clear picture of victory in his mind. He had gathered and sharpened his tools, equipping himself for the battle. Now he needed a plan, a set of steps that would take him from this point to victory. So David methodically charted the steps he planned to take and the sequence of actions he believed would lead to victory. In other words, he developed a strategic plan.

A strategic plan lays out the method to be used in order to achieve a particular goal. As you consider how to develop your plan, we would like to share three simple warnings. President Calvin Coolidge provides an illustration of the first.

Coolidge once invited friends from his hometown to dine with him at the White House. Unsure of their table manners, the guests decided to imitate the president. They watched closely to see which utensils he used, what foods he ate, and when. Their strategy seemed to succeed until coffee was served. Coolidge poured some coffee into his saucer. They did the same. He added sugar and cream. His guests did too. Then the president bent over and put his saucer on the floor for the cat! The first warning is this: Be careful whose example you follow; mimicking another will not lead to your own success. You must develop a plan that is based on your unique situation, not on someone else's.

Thomas Merton writes, "Action is the stream while contemplation is the spring." Contemplation is an element of the development of a strategy, and it is one that we tend to skip over. Many consider strategic planning a process that is only important for businesses or other organizations. But each of us must develop strategies throughout our lives. If we do not pause to contemplate our plans, we end up planning by default, moving through life in response-and-react mode, rather than operating from an overarching strategic plan. Contemplation will take time, but be warned that when you rush ahead without thoughtful consideration and contemplation, you imperil the rest of your plans. Make time to step back and take a long, deep look at your objectives, the reasons behind your efforts, not just the tasks ahead of you.

As we face difficult situations, strategy becomes more critical. Most individuals do not have a clear strategy for either their life in general or for specific situations. In fact, we are usually running, either from or to something. When we are on the run, making decisions only in response to our fears, we give fear the upper hand. We give fear power over our lives. We warn you not to live out of fear. When David faced Goliath, he looked around and realized everyone had left. His brothers and the other soldiers had run away. But David had a plan. Develop your plan as you face your giant. Take control of your own circumstances and decide to no longer to be at the mercy of whatever giant taunts you. Your strategic plan deflates the power of fear and provides a different way to move forward.

Why Strategy Matters

Business expert and consultant Jim Collins, in an interview with Charlie Rose, described a scenario regarding a nineteenth-century squadron of soldiers attempting to take a well-fortified position in battle. Their supplies were running low, including the gunpowder used for firing their weapons.

Their primary problem was that the conditions for battle were difficult, with foggy weather playing a significant role. It had become difficult for the artillery to correctly set the distance between the artillery base and the wall of the fort.

One commander of the attacking unit wanted to take the full load of gunpowder the unit had left and fire it at the wall. However, the executive officer knew that doing so would run the risk of wasting the whole of their supply of gunpowder in one slim chance for success. What if they missed? The executive officer devised a plan. He asked that smaller bullets be used as distance projectiles in order to measure the true trajectory of their firings. Not only would this approach conserve gunpowder but it would give them more chances to refine their plan and raise their odds of successful impact against the wall.

After several small shell firings, which did little physical damage to the wall, the gunnery sergeant was able to adjust for the appropriate trajectory of the unit's cannons, until the smaller bullet firings were striking the wall with perfect consistency. At that point, the commander asked for all the gunpowder to be used in one massive firing. Because the artillery was now set to the exact trajectory, the massive cannonball struck the target perfectly, with full force. The wall was breached, and the advancing army made their way through the wall for the attack.

Why did David choose five stones from the riverbed? Scripture provides no real explanation for this detail. Theories abound, including one that suggests Goliath had four brothers and that David was preparing to take them all. However, a simpler explanation abides.

David knew what it meant to battle beasts that were larger and more dangerous than he. In fact, David states that he had already fought the lion and bear, and that he would treat Goliath

with the same response. Sure, David was confident and courageous. But he was also prepared. He knew that he would have
a chance to stay in the battle and to win *only* if he was prepared
with a good plan.

So, maybe David chose those five stones deliberately, for a
specific reason, as part of his plan. Five stones. Not six or seven
or eight. Perhaps as part of his careful planning, David had cal-
culated the distance between himself and the giant. Perhaps he
estimated the time it would take Goliath to close in on him, if
he missed his first shot, and his second, and his third. David
would then know how many shots and how much time he had
to slay the giant, and could plan and prepare accordingly, giving
himself a chance to stay in the fight and win.

Conquering giants requires being prepared, from before that
first shot to the end of the battle. If we are serious about standing
against the giants of our lives, we must also be serious about a
strategic plan that gives us the best possible chance for success.
The following principles will help you develop an effective plan.

Principle One: Build a Solid but Flexible Framework
(Brad Martin)

An effective strategic plan for battling giants begins with a
solid but flexible framework. This framework lays out the ba-
sics—the core elements of your plan. Constructing this framework requires time and commitment, good old-fashioned hard
work. As the basis for your strategy, this framework must be
well thought out, so that there are no major gaps or holes. It

must be flexible, however, so that it can adjust to the inevitable changes and unforeseen challenges ahead. And this framework must include specific actions and accountabilities. Otherwise, it's an idea, not a strategy.

The framework of your strategic plan should be marked with milestones, points at which measurements can be taken and adjustments can be made. My first political campaign certainly required a strategic plan, and I built that plan on a solid but flexible framework. Using the tools I had available and the picture I had drawn, I created a map of the legislative district in which I was running and planned the tally of votes by neighborhood, which would permit me to win the election. A core tactic in my plan was knocking on doors and putting up yard signs. I measured execution to the plan, based upon the number of houses I visited and the number of signs that were installed.

Once the polls closed on election day, my campaign team gathered to tally the results as they were reported from each precinct. As the numbers came in, we posted the actual results against our targets. With only one precinct yet to report, I was leading the race by two hundred votes, and we were awaiting the vote totals from the final precinct, which my plan indicated we would lose by three hundred votes. It was a bit somber in our headquarters until that last precinct was posted on the chart. But, rather than lose that neighborhood by three hundred votes, I actually won it by three hundred votes. So the plan wasn't perfect, but it was solid. We had taken the time to think it through, do our research, and cover all the bases. It included milestones and accountabilities. All of this created a framework for me to execute, upon which my efforts could be organized. It was indeed the basis of a winning strategy.

Lessons in Shortsightedness, or Why You Can't Build a Strong Plan on a Weak Framework

A solid plan requires hard work in its creation and accountability in its execution. I cannot emphasize this enough. Many people land on an idea and call it a plan. But a successful plan must be constructed methodically, piece-by-piece, or it will be fragile and fall apart before you've gotten anywhere close to conquering your giant. This is why we want you to think about the framework for your plan *first.* You can do this work quickly if necessary, as David surely did. But you cannot skirt around it. You can't say, I'll just grab my slingshot and run up there and kill that giant! without building a solid plan, and have any hope for success. Sometimes it helps to review lessons learned the hard way in life, and I have certainly experienced a few of those.

The American businessman, Boone Pickens, has been quoted as saying, "A plan without action is not a plan. It's a speech." The purchase of the Proffitt's department store business was a rather complicated proposition. We needed a plan to achieve it. But at the time I viewed the acquisition as a single project and didn't see far past the actual purchase itself. I hired outside accountants to develop binders of financial projections for presentation to banks to obtain financing. And that was my version of a plan for the department store business. While this exercise was helpful for getting the financing for the transaction, it was of no value when it came to the actual responsibility of operating the company. I soon learned that projections are very different from plans.

Your plan must be strong and as complete as possible, but it must also be flexible so that it allows you to adjust when some unexpected new giant appears on the horizon.

Just prior to the birth of our son, Myles, my wife and I attended a parent-to-be seminar hosted by the hospital where our son would be born. We spent six hours that day listening to health care professionals outline plans we should make to care for our new baby. As we left the seminar, I told Dina that I felt the staff had done a wonderful job of helping these soon-to-be-new parents build a plan to keep their child fed, clean, and safe. But my sense was that we probably could have figured out most of those things on our own. I did note, however, that if the attendees were an accurate statistical subset of similar parents-to-be, one could predict that within ten to fifteen years, half of the couples in the seminar would divorce. Their lives were about to change in a significant way with the addition of a child to their home. Yet nowhere in the seminar did we learn about the strains that can occur in the marriage as a result of such change. Nor did we spend any time building a plan for what would matter most to the long-term health and security of the child—being part of a loving, stable family.

I certainly did not plan for my first marriage to end in divorce. But it did happen, after twenty-four years. In retrospect, while I was making plans for my business, kids, homes, and community service, I did not have a strategy for my marriage. Life changes occurred, and I had not put in place the accountabilities that might have signaled that divorce would be a real threat in my future.

A strategic plan is essential in fighting your giants. If you begin with a strong and flexible framework and built-in milestones and accountabilities, you will have a stable foundation on which to stand. From there, you may see warning signs that a new giant is looming just beyond the horizon. Then, you'll be able to adjust some portion of your plan to meet and conquer that new giant.

Principle Two: Use Mentors
(Brad Martin)

We have seen that it takes work and commitment to build a good plan. For me, it is critical to have help in that effort. You can only see what *you* can see; another person's experience and skill provides important perspective and foresight. Whether you call them mentors, coaches, counselors, teachers, advisors, sages, or friends, you should ask for help from someone who is capable of aiding you in developing the plans for your battle.

A mentor can share experiences that he or she has lived through; you will benefit from their experiences without actually having to live through them, first-hand. A mentor can help you focus on what's most important in your strategy. A mentor can ensure that you are looking at a clear picture and speaking the truth to yourself—not ignoring a giant or minimizing its threat. And a mentor can show you a living example of one who has not only fought giants but survived those encounters.

When I was first running for the House of Representatives, I was a bit confused about how to most effectively communicate my campaign positions. I called upon Henry Loeb, the former mayor of Memphis and a man whom I had admired for years. When I sought his help about how to make my messages more appealing, Loeb quickly got to the point. "Don't worry about it. Just tell the truth," he said. "The voters might not like what they hear, but they will like *you.*"

When my first marriage was crumbling and I was struggling with what went wrong, I sought the counsel of John DeFoore, a therapist who became a mentor. I asked John what I needed to do to fix things, and he told me the cold hard truth. "Your marriage is over. Face the facts. Now get on with your life."

I could fill this entire book with accounts of mentors who have helped me achieve something of significance or endure something of difficulty. You will find that mentors will be available to you if you're willing to open up and ask for help and support. They will see that as a sign of strength, not weakness. The best leaders I have seen in business, politics, and families are inquisitive and personally secure enough to seek answers and help from others.

Many mentors certainly helped me along the way in the department store business, and my retail career would have been disastrous without their support.

My strategy for acquiring Proffitt's, a small department store chain headquartered in suburban Knoxville, Tennessee, was pretty straightforward. I planned to organize an investor group to buy the company, include its key managers as our partners, add value to it through its operations, and then, in the years ahead, sell it to one of the major chains in what I thought would become a consolidating industry. In the fall of 1984, aided by the support of two outstanding Memphis attorneys and mentors, Frank Watson Jr., and Bobby Cox, we acquired Proffitt's Incorporated for fourteen million dollars. Eleven million dollars of the purchase price was borrowed from a bank, and I personally guaranteed the bank loan. When people ask me today if I was worried about having to do so, I remind them that I didn't see that as a big problem. If things didn't work out, I didn't have eleven million to repay the bank anyway.

My intended role was to oversee the investment, not manage the department store business. But I had no retail-industry experience, and while I was audacious enough to organize the acquisition of the company and borrow a lot of money, I didn't quite know how to do so. That's when the founder of a great company and one of the investors in the Proffitt's acquisition asked if I had discussed Proffitt's with Edmond Cicala, a retired department-store executive who happened to live in my hometown of Memphis. "No, I had not thought of that," I replied. "Well," he said, "not talking to Ed Cicala about helping you with the department store business that you just bought would be like a guy buying a baseball team in Babe Ruth's hometown and not asking Babe if he had any suggestions for you."

I immediately sought a meeting with Mr. Cicala, told him about our recent acquisition, and asked if he would mentor me in the business. He began by asking a few direct and specific retail-industry questions. I had absolutely no idea what he was talking about, and he knew it. "I see you're going to need a lot of help," he nodded. Then Ed smiled at me and said, "I'm your man."

Ed Cicala mentored me in the fundamentals of the retail business and helped shape our strategy. I relied upon him for the next twenty years. I could not have succeeded without him as my coach.

Principle Three: Simplify
(Brad Martin)

Five years after the acquisition of Proffitt's, our strategy, and my role, had to change. The expected plan of selling the company to a bigger department store company was simply not going to materialize. Leveraged buyouts and operating miscues had impaired the ability of most of the prospective buyers to grow by acquisition, and they were, in fact, shrinking. The picture had changed. Furthermore, when our CEO abruptly retired, we needed a new strategy *and* a new CEO. The company was in debt, and so was I. It fell to me to assume the CEO responsibility and rethink strategy. Selling the company was not going to happen, so I decided we would grow.

While Ed Cicala had taught me the fundamentals of the department store business, no one had taught me how to run a large company. In addition to my CEO role, I became the head of merchandising of the company, another entirely new experience for me. In this additional new role, I had the responsibility of leading the company while learning its industry. Fortunately, my associates at Proffitt's were patient teachers and great partners.

As a first-time CEO, I initially found the level of responsibility to be a bit overwhelming, and I struggled with how to most effectively lead the company. The job I was trying to do seemed too complicated for me, so I decided I would have to simplify my focus.

I started by defining and communicating the values and standards by which the company would operate. These values became what we called our Four Cornerstones—Style, Quality, Service, and Integrity. Everything we would do would be based upon these four cornerstones. And to ensure that our employees and customers understood these standards, we literally dug up the floor at the center of each store and installed the Four Cornerstones in the floors of our buildings.

With a clear focus on our values and standards, next we had to clarify how our cornerstones would come to life in our business plans. A retail business is a detail business, so to help me allocate my time to the right details, I chose to be personally responsible and accountable for three areas of the business:

1. How we treat our customers

2. How we treat our employees

3. How the company grows

I counted on my associates to be responsible for everything else. They shared our values and were committed to the Four Cornerstones, and they did a remarkable job.

When I had the privilege of being named the CEO of Proffitt's, the company was generating seventy million dollars in revenues from ten stores in the eastern region of Tennessee. Through the extraordinary efforts and commitment of my special colleagues, ten years later, the company was known as Saks Incorporated, and its revenues were approximately seven billion dollars with over three hundred stores in the corporate family. As the CEO of the company, I certainly made many missteps and miscues along the way. And as a public company, we had significant visibility in the media, so these missteps were visible to all. There were times when I was praised in the business press as a visionary leader. On other occasions, I was described as "marginally incompetent"! The truth is that neither characterization was accurate. Like most of us, I was somewhere in the middle. The experience was often exciting, occasionally frightening, sometimes embarrassing, and, without a doubt, gratifying. And this was just my work, not my life.

During my eighteen-year tenure in the management of the company, our stock price grew by 1200 percent. When I share this story at business schools or leadership forums today, I'm often asked, "Did you feel like you were riding a rocket ship during this time?" "No," I reply. "It felt a lot more like a roller-coaster. But, I had the opportunity to ride the roller coaster with an extraordinary group of people. And it was, indeed, a great ride." So make your plan. Get help to do so. Keep it simple. Be accountable. And remember the difference between your work and your life.

Safe Cargo

Clovis Chappell, a minister from a century back, used to tell the story of two paddleboats. The boats left Memphis about the same time, traveling down the Mississippi River to New Orleans. As they traveled side-by-side, sailors from one vessel made a few remarks about the snail's pace of the other. Then, heated words were exchanged and challenges were made. And then, a race began. The competition became vicious as the two boats roared through the Deep South.

One boat began falling behind due to lack of fuel. There had been plenty of coal for the trip, but not enough for an outright race. As the boat dropped back, an enthusiastic young sailor took some of the ship's cargo and tossed it into the ovens. When the sailors saw that supplies burned as well as coal, they continued to fuel their boat with the very material they had been assigned to transport. They ended up winning the race but burned their cargo.

In life, and especially in fighting giants, it is easy to lose sight of our deepest, highest, truest priorities. Fighting giants is hard work and can be all consuming, taking every ounce of our personal fuel. As we do this work, we must remember that God has entrusted cargo to us too: children, spouses, and friends. Our job is to do our part in seeing that *this* precious cargo reaches its destination. When we forget this and fail to develop healthy priorities, the people around us suffer. Don't be tempted to sacrifice your cargo in order to achieve the number-one slot of your own selfish desires and objectives. Ensure that the precious cargo in your plan is delivered safely.

Are you truly ready to battle your giant? Or, would developing a strategic plan make the task easier? A plan will not mean your victory is certain, but it will mean that not only are you ready to fight but you are ready for wherever the fight may lead.

The Fourth Stone

YOUR TRAINING

TRAIN FOR VICTORY

"Knowing yourself is the beginning of all wisdom."
—*Aristotle*

"Your servant has kept his father's sheep," David replied to Saul, "and if ever a lion or a bear came and carried off one of the flock, I would go after it, strike it, and rescue the animal from its mouth. If it turned on me, I would grab it at its jaw, strike it, and kill it. Your servant has fought both lions and bears. This uncircumcised Philistine will be just like one of them because he has insulted the army of the living God.

"The LORD," David added, "who rescued me from the power of both lions and bears, will rescue me from the power of this Philistine."

—1 Samuel 17:34-37

Recently, we received the story of a ten-year-old boy who decided to study judo despite having lost his left arm in a devastating car accident.

An old Japanese judo master took the boy under his wing and began to train him. The boy was doing well but, after three months of training, couldn't quite understand why the old Master had taught him only one move.

"Sensei," the boy said, "Shouldn't I be learning more moves?"

The old master told the boy that though it was only one simple move, it would be the only move he would need. Though he didn't understand all the old master meant, the boy kept training.

Several months later, the old master took the boy to his first tournament. The boy easily won his first two matches. And, although the third match proved to be more difficult, his opponent became impatient and charged the boy. The boy used his one move and won that match as well. Amazed by his success, the boy advanced to the finals.

During the finals, the boy's opponent was bigger, stronger, and more experienced. No one believed the boy had a chance to defeat this latest challenge. Even the officials were concerned. The referee called a time-out and was about to stop the match when the boy's old master intervened. "No," the old master insisted, "let him continue."

"You can achieve victory. You have trained for this moment."

Soon after, the boy's opponent made a critical mistake. And, the boy used his one, special move to pin his opponent. The boy won the match and the tournament. He was the champion.

On the trip home, the boy and the old master reviewed every move in each and every match. Then the boy summoned the courage to ask what was really on his mind: "Old master, how did I win the tournament with only one move?"

"You won for two reasons," the old master answered. "First, you have nearly mastered one of the most difficult throws in all of judo. And second, the only known defense for that move is for your opponent to grab your left arm."

Have you ever known an elite athlete? One of the most impressive parts of their lives is watching their training schedules and routines. Now, the specifics may vary from athlete to athlete, especially depending on the sport or event.

However, according to most physical training experts, most athletes focus on five primary areas for training:

1. Specificity: Training for a specific skill or area of improvement requires performing exercises specific to those areas of targeted improvement.

2. Overload: A muscle will only increase its strength when pushed beyond its customary capacity, load, or intensity.

3. Recovery: To grow stronger also means to provide enough rest and opportunity for recovery to begin the strengthening process again.

4. Adaptation: The body will need time to adapt to the strengthening regimen. Adaptation begins with the recovery phase.

5. Consistency: This principle reminds the trainee that to stop training means to lose the growth and effect over time.

Thus, training is necessary to grow stronger for the task ahead. But, to grow stronger, we must first train wisely. And that requires a consistent, specific routine.

I (Brad) remember one of my first golf lessons with an outstanding local golf instructor. I hoped he could at least help me grasp the fundamentals of the game. In fact, that is where we started. However, early on things were not going well, and I grew frustrated with my lack of progress. Finally, after several failed attempts to strike the ball properly, I shouted, "Think, Brad, think!" To which the instructor replied, "No. . . . *Feel,* Brad, *feel.*"

With a consistent, focused training routine, you will begin to "feel" what you need to do. Don't underestimate the power of a consistent, focused training routine as the surest way to hone skills and develop expertise. This is true whether you are a world-class athlete or a faithful soldier facing the giants of this world.

The following principles for a spiritual training routine grow us stronger as we face the giants of life:

1. Sacrifice

2. Obedience

3. Effort

1) Sacrifice
(Shane Stanford)

Ms. Hattie worked as a housecleaner, seamstress, and laundry maid her entire life. She worked long, hard hours and her employers lived in another part of town, adding a long commute to her day. When she returned home, Ms. Hattie took care of her own family including six children, three boys and three girls. Ms. Hattie's husband passed away while their youngest child was still a baby. There was little rest for Ms. Hattie; there was no other choice.

Although materially Ms. Hattie never had very much, she was wealthy beyond measure. Ms. Hattie inherited the legacy of her family's faith and character, and she passed that legacy on to her children. She believed that with enough hard work and sacrifice, a person could achieve his or her goals. Ms. Hattie recognized the value of spiritual things as well, and she taught her children rich lessons about God's faithfulness. This type of wealth cannot be stolen, will never devalue, and will always provide generous dividends.

Ms. Hattie's oldest child was accepted to a small liberal arts college in South Carolina. The second child earned a scholarship to Vanderbilt University. The third child, the oldest son, went off to Brown University. Ms. Hattie's fourth and fifth children, twins, attended a large university in the northern part of their state. You wonder about her sixth child? He went to Harvard.

How does a seamstress send six kids to college? Through a life surrendered in sacrifice toward higher goals than the fleeting comforts this world offers. Such is the doorway to significance.

Ms. Hattie said that she learned sacrifice from her maternal grandmother, who was also a seamstress and the first generation of her family to live out of slavery. Ms. Hattie's grandmother used hard work as a means to give her family dignity and provide the needed resources to inch herself ever closer to opportunity. It may not have seemed like much at the time, and it certainly did not happen quickly; but eventually, Ms. Hattie's grandmother taught her valuable lessons about giving yourself to a purpose much greater than your own interests. Ms. Hattie passed those lessons down to her own children.

As Ms. Hattie's health began to fail, several of her children invited her to come live with them. Being a homebody, however, she chose to remain in the little community where she was born and had lived her whole life. She would always say, "I was born here, and I will die here."

Ms. Hattie died at the age of ninety-two. At the time of her death she still worked part-time as a seamstress, and she still was very active in her church. She also attended a local card game until just weeks prior to her death, and she continued to save her money and encourage others. When Ms. Hattie died, her banker contacted her children and asked them to gather at the bank to discuss their mother's will. The document stated that 10 percent of her estate should go to her church. She gave another 10 percent of her estate to various community ministries, including her former high school, which the school used to start a new library fund.

Ms. Hattie left the remainder of her estate to a local shelter ministry. Her children did not receive any funds, and not one of them protested. Their mother had told them early on what she was planning to do, and had reminded them that she had already given them the most important gifts she could provide: faith in God, strong relationships, encouragement, love, and the opportunity to achieve their full potential.

Ms. Hattie's estate was valued at nearly four hundred thousand. No one knew that Ms. Hattie had saved such an extraordinary amount of money—well, no one except her banker and pastor. They had both watched Ms. Hattie live a life of frugality so that others might benefit after she was gone. When her television broke, she saved for more than a year to pay for repairs to fix it. When her shoes started looking worn and frayed, she kept wearing them until, literally, the soles fell off. When she needed a dress for some event, instead of buying a new one, she wore the same hand-mended dress she had worn for years.

Ms. Hattie gave her life as a holy and living sacrifice, and she wanted her resources to count for something more than an impulsive purchase in the moment. One of her attorneys remarked after her death, "Ms. Hattie could have lived a completely different life than she had known, but instead, she chose to live her life in her manner. The result was a very wealthy life, not measured by money but by the kind of wealth the world cannot take away."

2) Obedience
(Shane Stanford)

At first glance, Chris is quiet and unassuming. To many, Chris is a staff member at a local church, a dedicated servant who remains quiet behind the scenes while others receive the glory. However, there is more than meets the eye when it comes to this faithful brother in Christ. Chris doesn't just talk about loving Jesus; he shows it with every aspect of his heart and life. An engineer with an MBA, Chris left his job of eighteen years to enter church ministry as the business administrator for a church. A couple of years later, Chris founded a mission ministry that takes recreation to children in under-resourced areas from the

Ninth Ward of New Orleans to the slums of Costa Rica. To many of us, Chris is a modern-day saint who embodies the best of what being the "hands and feet of the gospel" means. Chris uses his administrative skills to guide and build teams that make a difference in their communities and beyond. The most important part of Chris's witness is his obedience. He had a good life, a safe life. But, he heard God calling him to something more. And, this one man left everything he knew to make a difference and to be obedient to what God called him to do.

In the biblical book named for him, James says, "Come near to God, and he will come near to you..." (4:8). This verse is largely misread as an ultimatum from God. But nothing could be further from the truth. Instead, the Scripture offers some common-sense wisdom. How do you embrace someone who refuses to open his or her arms? How can you look deeply into someone's eyes when that person refuses to make eye contact? How do you truly know someone who refuses to let you into his or her heart and life? Scripture tells us that God is always near. God is not the problem. The real question is whether we will draw near to God.

We must follow where God leads, even when the situation is uncomfortable and difficult. Obedience leads us beyond what we can see or understand. Obedience happens when we commit ourselves to a closer walk with God. Obedience is not meant to be hard or difficult. In fact, it should be an outflow of what God has planted inside of us. The challenge in obedience lies in being able to wade past the world's other requirements and in redefining the nature of how we are called to make a difference.

We often set up our lives trying to satisfy others, when it is God's satisfaction that really matters.

On a Sunday afternoon in March of 2005, I received an emergency call at my home in Memphis stating that my oldest son was unconscious and en route by ambulance to a hospital in New York. I rushed to the airport, quickly flew to New York City, and arrived at the ICU of the hospital to learn that he was a victim of an accidental overdose of prescription drugs. My son was breathing but unconscious, and a number of his important vital signs were of grave concern. I tried to assist in the organization of his medical treatment but was essentially helpless, and ultimately I had to trust the professionals who were providing his care.

My son was transported by ambulance the next morning to another hospital with more extensive resources for his care. He remained unconscious and unresponsive. My friends and family provided enormous support to me during this terrifying time, but there was nothing we could do except to pray and hope. This was a giant I never expected our family to face; and in a waiting room in the ICU, in my hotel room, and in the taxicab back and forth to the hospital, I literally clung to a Bible I had grabbed as I left my home in Memphis. I looked to specific verses and chapters in the book for strength and for the ability to comfort others who were also in pain. And I prayed for the medical team that was attempting to save my son's life.

My son remained unconscious throughout the next four days. On Thursday evening, my family took a break from the hospital to attend an Easter week service at a local church. I could not focus on the service, as my mind constantly returned to the hospital and the condition of my son. Yet in the midst of the singing of a hymn, my eyes wandered about the sanctuary and were drawn to a beautiful stained glass window that depicted Jesus Christ, arms outstretched and palms open. The eyes of the figure in the window were locked upon mine, and the message to me was very clear. "You give me your heart, your mind, and your attention," Christ was saying. "Obey Me. Have faith in me. I am with your son. Be here with me."

After the church service that night, I received an e-mail from my wonderful sister-in-law, Marika, reminding me to have faith and citing Mark 9:29. "And He said unto them, 'This kind [of demon] can come out only by prayer'" (NIV). And, pray so many did.

The following morning, my son opened his eyes and awoke from a nearly one-week coma. And he began a journey of recovery under God's watchful eye.

As I reflect eight years later on this crisis, I realize that I grabbed my Bible and found myself in the sanctuary of a local church instinctively. The Bible and sanctuary were my first impulse after years of spiritual routine. These were the tools that I relied upon to take the steps personally to be in a relationship with God. And while I had no guarantee of the outcome of this crisis, I can't imagine facing that kind of giant without God's sustaining, strengthening, peace-giving presence.

3) Effort
(Shane Stanford)

It was 1993 at the National Cherry Blossom Festival and ten-mile run in Washington, D.C. Though I am not a runner, I attended the festival for the express purpose of seeing the Kenyan long-distance running team compete in the race. It is a thrill to watch this team! You don't need to be a runner to appreciate the incredible skill it takes to do what these athletes do. And they almost make it look easy. The Kenyan team was, at the time, the best long-distance team in the world. In the running world, they were the stuff of legends. The Kenyan runners' tenacity, speed, and dominance propelled them beyond their competitors. The fact that many of them ran in bare feet only increased the aura of amazement among the spectators that witnessed them.

The Kenyan team's running technique seemed to be more art than athleticism. They approached their sport with the same fervor and dedication as other athletes, but there seemed to be something spiritual about the way they used their gifts. Many said that they were born for this purpose—for running with this level of excellence, on this world platform. After watching the Kenyans that day, I couldn't agree more.

The Kenyan team ran with passion as though they did not carry just their own hopes and dreams but also the aspirations of everyone from their country. They ran with spirit and focus and technical perfection. The Kenyan team redefined the sport. They ran because, as they would later note, they loved it.

Research deeper into the Kenyan team's habits and history, and you will see that their success resulted from the same crucial element that all successful endeavors credit: effort. These runners didn't just live off of passion; no one can sustain excellence with passion alone. Instead, they channeled their love of the sport into effort—hours of practice and hard work. They knew their passion and gifts had given them an edge, but they also knew that they would have to work hard and be more focused than anyone else in order to be the best.

There is a divine flow to our lives, whether in athletic, intellectual, or relational pursuits, when developing our gifts and using them in the manner that God intended intersects perfectly. But that flow only happens when we employ what we have been given, when we recognize our gifts and then put forth effort to use them well.

We have all known people who seem to be in the background, who are perceived to have little influence when judged by the world's standards. But when offered a chance to employ their gifts in some way, the power and impact of their efforts can be astonishing. A person who is gifted in hospitality, for instance, can make the most hesitant person feel welcome in a strange, new setting. This is no small feat, and it happens when gifts and effort are aligned. The world around you will try to designate which gifts are "important" and which are not. You may not be a world-class athlete. Your photo will probably never appear on the cover of *Sports Illustrated*. But you are gifted, nonetheless. Recognize your gifts, and put forth the effort required to train and develop them so that you can use those gifts well.

Perhaps no one embraced the intersection of faith and effort more completely than the Apostle Paul. Paul is the most significant practical theologian in Christian history—practical being the most important word to define him. He believed that faith came through belief in Christ alone, but the power of faith came to life in our efforts to live faithfully for Christ in the world. To articulate this passionate view of faith, Paul described his journey as the effort of a world-class athlete. And, to achieve the prize or win the race, one must train. Paul states,

> Not that I have already obtained all this, or have already been made perfect, but I press on to take hold of that for which Christ Jesus took hold of me. Brothers, I do not consider myself yet to have taken hold of it. But one thing I do: Forgetting what is behind and straining toward what is ahead, I press on toward the goal to win the prize for which God has called me heavenward in Christ Jesus.
> All of us who are mature should take such a view of things. (Philippians 3:12-15a NIV)

The Apostle Paul's words to the church at Philippi are about gratitude, hard work, and living up to our potential. They are also about effort in leadership and keeping focused on the good work that God has placed in our lives.

Paul is "running a race" to live out what God has gifted inside of him (see 1 Corinthians 9:24–25). Paul characterized it as a race, and he knew it was his job to run it to the best of his ability—to win it. This would require Paul to give his best—to live a sacrificial, obedient, and mature life. But, as Paul said to the Philippians, all of this will get you only so far. "All of us who are mature," he says, "will have to go the extra mile. We will have to put forth incredible effort."

Not once, but twice Paul gives the image of straining and effort to do that which God had placed in his life. He says that he presses on (Philippians 3:12), and that he is "straining toward what is ahead" (3:13 NIV). Then, almost as if to reiterate the cheer, Paul says again, "I press on toward the goal to win the prize" (3:14 NIV). How important is this part of the process for Paul? Look at the last verse in this passage: "All of us who are mature should take such a view of things" (3:15 NIV). Being mature means putting forth effort. If we don't put forth that effort, Paul says, then we are not as mature as we had thought.

This is not just a pep talk. These are Paul's words to people he loves, about the work given to him by the God he loves. This is a heart-to-heart message—a locker room speech that says to those in training, today is game day! The legendary coach of the Green Bay Packers, Coach Vince Lombardi, is often quoted as saying, "Victory is not everything; it's the only thing." When fighting a giant, winning is the only thing. Train that way.

The Fifth Stone

YOUR NERVE

Run Boldly to Meet the Giant

> *"Boldness be my friend."*
> —*Cymbeline, William Shakespeare*

> The Philistine got up and moved closer to attack David, and David ran quickly to the front line to face him. David put his hand in his bag and took out a stone. He slung it, and it hit the Philistine on his forehead. The stone penetrated his forehead, and he fell face down on the ground.
>
> —1 Samuel 17:48-49

David was ready for the battle. He did not hesitate. With abundant courage and amazing nerve, he ran boldly to meet the giant.

A Bold Life

In 2007, I (Shane) had the privilege of sharing keynote responsibilities at a World AIDS Day event with Jeanne Hale, mother of AIDS activist and victim Ryan White. Ryan was born a few months after me. He died at the age of eighteen after a hard and much-publicized battle with the disease. He had been prevented from registering for school in the Indiana town where he grew up in the 1980s. The news outlets jumped at the chance to chronicle the fight, which, at the time, was only one of the public struggles throughout the country over the rights of AIDS victims and of hemophiliacs. The story drew a great deal of attention and made Ryan an instant celebrity. It also brought him new friends in such noted public figures as Elton John, Michael Jackson, and Elizabeth Taylor.

Ryan fought a valiant fight and became an example to everyone in the battle and all those living with the disease. His life served as an example to all of us. Ryan, though just a young boy when he began his fight against AIDS, not only carried himself with dignity but also became a role model for how to deal with difficult choices and places in our lives. People were amazed that this young teenage boy could show such maturity, strength, and courage in the face of great opposition—opposition both from the disease and from others.

Although our paths never crossed, being so close in age I felt as though I knew Ryan; I think everyone fighting AIDS or who was close to the issue in some way felt as though they knew him. Ryan fought his battle with HIV in the public eye. I, like many others, fought the battle privately. I remember watching Ryan's public battle and wondering what the strain of the limelight meant for him. I would learn later that Ryan had the same aspirations, fears, and challenges as other boys our age. It was just that his story played out on television screens and through the lens of a camera.

That night in 2007 at the World AIDS Day conference, Ryan White's mother, Jeanne, and I spent time talking about those days before the world "got on board" in the fight against AIDS and before the host of medicines used to treat people and to save lives were available. Those were difficult times, but a few people courageously stood up for those whom the Scriptures refer to as "the least of these."

Ryan was a champion in the fight at a time when AIDS was a death sentence and when disclosing one's condition did not elicit sympathy as much as suspicion, fear, and prejudice. There were no medical treatments, and little was known of the disease. Ryan stepped into the storm with bravery and maturity that astounded all those who watched. His life became a symbol of courage and strength that inspired a nation, and he paved the way for so many of us with the disease.

Our level of maturity, in large part, defines our ability to move forward not only in what God has given us to accomplish but also in how we face the difficulties along the way.

For now we are alive if you are standing your ground in the Lord. How can we thank God enough for you, given all the joy we have because of you before our God? Night and day, we pray more than ever to see all of you in person and to complete whatever you still need for your faith. Now may our God and Father himself guide us on our way back to you. May the Lord cause you to increase and enrich your love for each other and for everyone in the same way as we also love you. May the love cause your hearts to be strengthened, to be blameless in holiness before our God and Father when our Lord Jesus comes with all his people. (1 Thessalonians 3:8-15)

As Paul saw, most of the followers' struggles were not a result of their inability to stand firm but their inability to grow from their times of struggle. In his second letter to the church at Thessalonica, Paul tells them to "stand firm" in their struggles and to hold fast to what he had taught them (2 Thessalonians 2:13–15). This wasn't so that they would remain in the same spiritual place but so that they would, over the course of their relationship in Christ, grow deeper in their faith. Idleness leads to all sorts of other struggles, Paul insists, with the most severe being a spiritual apathy.

Growing deeper—gaining maturity—provides the roots by which obedience becomes a way of life. Faith, much like a tree, grows up and out in relation to how deeply it has planted its roots.

As we grow deeper in our relationship with God, our gifts become more vital. The more vital our gifts, the more God works in and through our lives, using our resources to do significant things—like taking down giants. Growing deeper in our walk with God is not easy. Maturity is the "game changer" for how effectively we use our gifts. The deeper we grow, the stronger we are.

We live in a world where a person's every move can be analyzed or debated. We too often feel entitled to the many blessings we receive, so much so that when the giants *do* appear, we look to everyone but ourselves as the one who will stop giants from trespassing into our lives. Sometimes, the world does not make sense. There is no clear path to victory. And, the giants often do cause much damage and heartache.

When the giants do arise, someone must be bold enough— without explanation or discussion—to take up the cause. Someone must look to the horizon and move *toward* the giant. When David arrived at camp and saw how his own family cowered behind their tents, afraid of Goliath, he knew that they had chosen to act more like the other side of the clan. That would be how people without faith act, and live, and respond. David chose to reflect something better, something more that day, and that led him boldly to face the giant once and for all. No matter what he had asked of his brothers in the army, or what the king had offered, or what his father had prayed, there came a time when David, the shepherd, ran boldly to meet the giant.

Running Boldly to Meet the Giant

We'd like to offer two principles that we have found to be important for running boldly to meet the giant.

First, *running boldly begins with having the confidence that you are prepared.* The great head coach for the Dallas Cowboys, Tom Landry, was fond of saying perfection is execution. Coach Landry was one of the most disciplined and ordered coaches in all of football. The creator of the Flex Defense and the multi-shifting backfield of the modern NFL offense, Landry believed that principles, preparation, and practice determined the success of a team long before they ever hit the field. A team was only as strong and as able on the field as the values and discipline instilled into each player before game day. The more prepared a team was, the more boldly they could play.

Sun Tzu, Chinese warrior leader of 450 BC, wrote, "Every battle is won before it is fought." Truly, when it comes to meeting the giants in our lives, we are as bold as we are prepared.

Second, *running boldly happens with complete commitment.* A man was walking along the edge of a steep cliff when he lost his footing and tumbled over. He managed to grab a branch protruding from the side of the mountain. He held on, looked heavenward and yelled, "Is anyone up there? Can anyone help me?"

After a few quiet moments, a voice from the sky responded, "I am here!"

The man, stunned but also relieved, said, "Oh, thank you, I am so glad to hear your voice. What should I do to receive your help?"

The voice replied, "Let go."

The man, thinking he had heard a mistake, said, "What was that?"

The voice again said, "In order for me to help you, you must let go."

The man was quiet for the next few moments. Finally, the man said, "Is anyone else up there?"

At a certain point, David's preparation had to stop. He could train no more. Suddenly, he found himself on the battlefield. There were no more conversations about strategy or focus.

It was time to fight. And when that time came, it required complete commitment.

When Julius Caesar landed on the shores of Britain with his Roman legions, he took a bold and decisive step to ensure the success of his military venture. Ordering his men to march to the edge of the Cliffs of Dover, he commanded them to look down at the water below. To their amazement, they saw every ship in which they had crossed the channel engulfed in flames. Caesar had deliberately cut off any possibility of retreat. Now that his soldiers were unable to return to the continent, there was nothing left for them to do but to advance and conquer! And that is exactly what they did.

Are you prepared to fight? Have you planned and trained? Is your path of attack clear? John H. Holcomb, author of *The Militant Moderate*, once wrote, "You must get involved to have an impact. No one is impressed with the won-lost record of the referee." You can't stand on the sidelines and win the game at the same time. Now is the time to look at the enemy and attack.

Door-to-Door
(Brad Martin)

The strategy of my first race for the House of Representatives was to campaign door-to-door, introduce myself to voters, and ask for their support. My goal was to knock on the door of virtually every house in the district, and I trudged through the neighborhoods hour after hour, day after day doing so. About three weeks before the election, knowing I had many neighborhoods yet to visit, I was wearing down and ready to call it a day.

I made one more stop, knocked on the door, and was greeted by a woman and her disabled daughter. I delivered my standard message that I was running for the House of Representatives and would appreciate her vote. She invited me into her home, and after introducing me to her daughter she talked about the challenges of finding services for her deaf and intellectually disabled child. She expressed frustration and indeed despair, and asked if I were elected what would I do to help her daughter? I walked out of her living room that night with no specific plan for what I might be able to do for her family and others in similar situations. But I knew that I had to help, and if I were to have the opportunity to do so, there were thousands more homes to visit and votes to seek. From that night on, I literally ran door-to-door.

Giants are risky, and fear is often associated with risk. But boldness will overcome that paralyzing fear. Whether it's a relationship to repair, a career opportunity to pursue, or a health giant to combat, follow the example of David. Run boldly.

SURVIVING THE BATTLE

BY BRAD MARTIN

My first marriage of over twenty years ended in divorce. Throughout the marriage, I certainly never drew a picture of failure or anticipated that it would end, but after the marriage was over, for a period, I did in fact view it as failure. During this difficult time, I visited a counselor for the first time in my life and watched in amazement as this professional drew a time-line of the significant events of my adulthood. While I had focused on expanding business activities as well as a myriad of other responsibilities and activities with my children throughout this timeframe, I had not truly considered the impact of many life changes that occurred during these years. I did not recognize the changes in the picture as they materialized, and I did not build a framework to address the challenges associated with these changes. For this reason, these natural life changes took a cumulative toll on the marriage. By the time I found myself wondering, what's wrong with this picture? or, what have I done wrong? it was simply too late. I should have noticed the picture was changing over the years and, like an oil painting, touched up and tended to its image as necessary.

My initial tendency during tough times is to "paint a pretty picture." But some pretty pictures are outright frauds. When divorce became inevitable, I turned from painting a pretty picture to "making the best of it"—also known as pretty picture's close cousin. And in order to make the best of it, I prepared notes to follow on the miserable occasion when I would have to tell our sons that their parents were getting divorced, and I reviewed these notes with my counselor. The notes began with the statement, "Your parents are going to divorce, but everything will be all right." After reading this line, my counselor interrupted me with the harsh command, "DO NOT LIE TO THEM! Everything is NOT going to be all right. Everything is going to be miserable. Tell them the truth. Then deal with it." When the time came to speak with my sons, I did choose to share the authentic picture of our family's situation, and we all set about the hard work of dealing with it.

Divorce is a giant. I did not picture confronting this giant, nor did I win the battle against it. But I *did* survive the encounter. Sometimes surviving the battle is the best we can do. Surviving means we get another chance. And while I was wounded in this battle, as I healed I became stronger than ever before.

Take a Step

There is a story about a Peruvian woman who was in charge of getting water for her village. An American journalist writing about the customs of the community to which the woman belonged arrived in the village and quickly became enthralled with the many unique experiences of the villagers. One of the customs was their process of gathering water. The villagers had access to one well that was eleven miles away on a road to a neighboring village. A group of women in the village woke before dawn every morning to walk the eleven miles carrying large ceramic vases to bring water from the well. The journalist watched this ritual unfold every morning of every day.

The journalist was amazed by the dedication of this group of women. They never complained, never uttered a single word indicating discomfort or weariness. They simply gathered their vases and went to the well.

After watching the women return one day from their journey, the journalist went to the women and asked, "How is it that you do this every day? How is it possible that you are able to repeat this task time and time again?"

The women looked at the journalist with great confusion. Finally, one of the women, who appeared to be their leader, stepped forward and said, "You ask how we are able to do this each and every day?"

"Yes" the journalist replied.

The woman, looking to the road and then back at the journalist, said, "Each morning, we watch for the sunrise, and we know that our village will need water that day. And, so, we rise and meet at the center of the village, gather our vases, turn our faces toward the road, and walk...and walk...and walk." The journalist smiled and then nodded his head, as though to agree with the woman.

The journalist knew that the woman was not being sarcastic or rude. No, her world, her village needed water. And, in order to have water, someone must take up the cause. *Thus, she gathers her vase, turns her eyes to the road, and walks.* This story may seem simplistic, but there is power and boldness in its simplicity.

This book asks you to take that first step toward conquering your giants. Maybe one step is all you have in you at this point. But, one step is enough. Don't let the giant win because you are afraid to move or because you remain hidden behind your fear. Haven't the giants taken enough from you? God can work with one simple step.

A Chance for Greatness

John Hunter is a fourth grade public school teacher in Charlottesville, Virginia, founder of the World Peace Game, and a fellow at The Martin Institute for Teaching Excellence at Presbyterian Day School in Memphis. What began nearly thirty years ago as John's creative way to teach fourth graders problem solving and conflict resolution skills, the World Peace Game has become a resource that has been used at the United Nations and the Pentagon and that has inspired thousands of other teachers to create similar vehicles to enrich the educational experience of their students. John stands outside the school where he teaches each day greeting students as they exit their vehicles in the carpool line. "Good morning," he cheerfully greets each student, "Here goes another chance for greatness."

And that's what we believe awaits you. You have a chance for greatness. No giant need block your way.

Second Chance

In the winter of 2002, I was traveling extensively for my responsibilities for Saks and was only occasionally in my hometown of Memphis. One evening I found myself home with no plans or prior commitments, and I decided at the last minute to go by myself to a Memphis Grizzlies basketball game.

I wandered in during the middle of the first quarter, watched some hoops, and at half time lined up in the concession line. That's when I noticed a beautiful woman in the same line who was speaking with the wife of a friend of mine. In what I'm certain was a very clumsy way, I managed to say "Hi" and learn that this extraordinary lady's name was Dina, and to talk with her for a couple of minutes in the lobby of the arena. As we returned to our respective seats, I asked if she and her friend were going somewhere after the game, and they said they were probably going to stop by a popular local restaurant. "Oh," I fibbed, "I was planning to go there too. Maybe we will run into each other."

At the end of the game I left with no idea of the final score and drove around killing time for about thirty minutes before I "casually" showed up at the restaurant. Once I saw Dina, I quickly elbowed my way to a seat nearby so I might engage her in conversation. After that evening, we decided we might hang out some together, perhaps be friends, but we did not arrange to officially date. That changed a few months later when I realized while I was travelling the world, engaged in interesting business challenges and interacting with fascinating people, that I missed her—I missed her *a lot*. Something was happening to my picture.

Soon after meeting Dina, I knew she was remarkable. I later heard that she was musically talented as well. In the summer of 2002, Dina invited me to attend a performance of *The Bouffants*, a popular band of which she was a member. I returned from a trip to Australia just in time to attend her show at a local restaurant and nightclub. Bedraggled from twenty-four hours of travel, I appeared at the club and made my way to an open seat at the bar. As I glanced around the restaurant, I saw a number of friends and acquaintances who looked at me and then quickly averted their eyes. They were probably thinking, "Poor Brad, look what it's come to for him—alone on Saturday night in a bar. What a sad picture." Little did I care what they thought once the band came out and I heard Dina sing—I was further down the path of no return.

Dina and I spent a lot of time together that fall and winter and discussed the possibility of marriage. We attended church, saw counselors, and cemented relationships with our respective friends and families. We decided to marry on the eleventh of October in East Tennessee (aka Big Orange country for the beloved Tennessee Volunteers), near our home at Blackberry Farm. Before deciding on a date, we approached the pastor of Campground Methodist Church, average Sunday attendance thirty, and asked for permission to marry on a particularly revered day in his church. The pastor's immediate and natural response was, "But that's the day of the Tennessee/Georgia football game." After some negotiation, we were granted permission to have our wedding at the church on the same day as the game. We had a better day that Saturday in 2003 than the Volunteers, and Dina and I began a new phase of life together.

The portrait of my life today includes my beautiful wife, three young sons, two grown sons, two daughters-in-law, and four grandchildren. It is a beautiful and rich picture. This picture was not one I had contemplated or expected to draw. Instead, God drew it for me. I simply had to care for and appreciate it. This was our chance for greatness.

One day I told my brother, Brian (perhaps the wisest person I know), I just didn't envision how great this new picture could be. "Of course, it can be great," he replied, "You only get married for the second time once."

Big Enough

One of my early mentors was the former mayor of Memphis, Henry Loeb. Henry and I often had different political views, but I always admired his integrity and courage. Henry served as mayor during a very difficult time in 1968, when Dr. Martin Luther King, Jr., was assassinated in my hometown.

The "public" Henry Loeb was well documented, but few knew that, in a private way, Loeb was an extraordinary friend to many who were downtrodden and to those with challenging disabilities as well. To see this powerful and physically imposing public man privately and quietly help so many who lived under circumstances that were so different from his own left a lasting mark on me.

A number of years after his death, upon the occasion of naming a building at Lambuth College in Jackson, Tennessee, in honor of Loeb, his family asked me to speak on their behalf. I made some brief remarks and was followed on stage by Hollis Leggett, a remarkable entrepreneur and benefactor of Lambuth. I was one of the few people in the audience that day who knew that Henry had been there for Hollis decades before, when Hollis was facing his own giant.

Hollis's remarks that afternoon were unforgettable. "When Henry Loeb passed away, a local television reporter interviewed a man who had been one of Henry's staunchest political adversaries during much of their respective public lives. When asked for one final comment about Loeb, his rival said, 'Henry and I never agreed on much of anything, but I will say one thing about him. He really cared for the little people.'"

Hollis shook his head side to side and in a soft voice concluded, "That was one more example of a person who never understood Henry. To Henry Loeb, there were no 'little people.'"

You are big enough to face any giant. God does not make "little people."

Jesus Is Here

During the Christmas season a few years ago, I was running some late errands with my three young sons in the family van. We had one final stop to make—deliver Christmas gifts to the Missionaries of Charity home in Memphis. The Missionaries of Charity are, of course, the worldwide ministry established by the great Mother Teresa. In Memphis, they quietly go about serving God through caring for women in difficult transitions and with special needs.

As I was unloading packages from the car that evening, focused on my final task of the day, my four-year-old son, Wesley, called out from the back seat of the van, "Dad, Jesus is here." I smiled and said back to him, "Of course, Jesus is here. This is Mother Teresa's place." I continued to gather items from the trunk when again Wesley called out, "No, Dad, Jesus is HERE."

"I know," I replied, perhaps a bit wearily, "This is a mission. These ladies are nuns. Of course Jesus is here." Wesley looked at me clearly puzzled. He had probably never heard the words "mission" or "nun" before. Undeterred, Wesley then climbed out of the van, grabbed my hand, and walked me over to the garden of the home and said with excitement, "Look, Dad, Jesus, is RIGHT HERE." And, indeed, there he was. In the garden was a two-foot statute of Jesus. I just had to take time to notice. So now, look at your picture!

Grab your tools.

Follow your strategy.

Train relentlessly.

Start walking.

Soon you will run boldly.

You are big enough.

And know as you go to battle, you are not alone.

Jesus is here.

The Training Manual

Before and While You Train

No one should proceed into battle without being prepared. And no one appropriately prepares for battle without training for victory. The Training Manual is a five-week study and devotional guide that will help to align your heart with God's, as you focus your spiritual formation on the task at hand—confronting the giants of your life. Other spiritual formation journeys will shape your prayer and devotional life, but facing giants—preparing for certain battles or difficult endeavors—requires a special period of training and development.

The following training regimen prepares you for taking up the *Five Stones* in your life and transforming them into weapons for battle. The process also shapes you through consistent study of the Scriptures, prayer focus, and study questions that challenge and stretch your faith *and* faithfulness.

The regimen is divided into two forms: your weekly objectives and your daily tasks. Each is important for the overall goal—becoming stronger and more confident in your faith and spiritual life. The weekly objectives are arranged around each of the five stones. Each week you will focus on developing your confidence in the use of that particular stone. The daily devotional provides consistent reinforcement for your weekly objective. Like a physical training regimen, our spiritual development and confidence develops in stages—not all at once. And spiritual muscle memory, a concept we consider very important, only evolves through consistent application and study.

So, a few suggestions before you start—

1. **Scripture.** Make sure you have a Scripture translation that allows for easy understanding but is also an accurate translation of the Hebrew and Greek texts. There are many translations that are world-class, and any one of them will be sufficient. We recommend the Common English Bible, because we have found this rather new translation to be incredibly accurate and usable.

2. **Consistency.** Provide for as much consistency in your setting and time of study as possible. Many people find devotional and study routines difficult because of inconsistency. We realize that no one can set his or her routine in cement. However, the more stable the routine, the more stable the lessons. The regimen follows a specific process. Each week begins with Discover, where you'll explore what is it that God needs you to "discover" to best apply this Stone to your fight. The next section is entitled Deepen. Here you will use the daily Scriptures, prayers, and focus questions to develop your confidence in who God is calling you to be and what God is calling you to do. Finally, at the end of the

training manual, we will challenge you to *Disciple* someone else in their fight against the giant of their lives. What have you learned about loving Jesus that allows you to *love like* Jesus in the world?

3. **Journal.** Many Christians do not utilize the incredibly important tool of journaling in their spiritual development. In many ways, Scripture is the journaling process between God and humanity. God loves to write things down for us to learn. And God has given us the gift of walking back through our own journaling to see the evidence of God's work and answers to prayers. When confronting our giants, that evidence is worth its weight in gold for building confidence for the next part of the fight.

4. **Community.** We do not believe that Christians walk alone for this journey. We are created by a God who values relationship (Genesis 1-3) and we find relationships stamped throughout Scripture as a valuable part of how we not only love Jesus but love like Jesus. Find a prayer partner, a study group, or just a sounding board for sharing the journey. We don't believe David decided to walk into this fight alone. He did so only after no other options presented themselves.

5. **The Writing on the Wall Test.** We recommend a tool that may sound strange but that we have found to be important. We believe many of you may be

reading this book during a crucial stage in your life. Many years ago, I (Shane) began a process of growing my spiritual confidence, especially when facing a specific task. I took the scriptural passage or set of scriptural passages that I believed God had put in my path, printed them out, and taped them to the wall to read daily. So, for every new scripture you encounter in this training regimen, we suggest you also keep 1 Samuel 17 in front you. God has placed the story of David and Goliath in your path for a reason. Pin it to your wall, learn from it, and allow the unique message that God needs to say to you to unfold each day.

DRAW A CLEAR PICTURE

Discover: Your task this week is to draw a clear picture of the outcome you seek when confronting the giant of your life. On day one, using a blank piece of paper, draw something that represents the outcome you seek. You can draw an image, use words, make a diagram—whatever helps you to visualize the giant after you've defeated it. Don't worry about style or artistic value. The objective is to get something on paper, and then to shape it throughout the week as you deepen your journey. Remember, God is unveiling this picture to you as your proximity to God changes. The closer you grow toward God, the clearer the picture becomes. We not only want you to see the final product, we believe the ongoing development teaches important lessons as well.

Deepen: Each day, faithfully and consistently work through each Scripture passage, the focus questions, and prayer.

Day One:

Scripture: Proverbs 3:5-6
Trust in the LORD with all your heart;
*   don't rely on your own intelligence.*
Know him in all your paths,
and he will keep your ways straight.

Training Principle: To draw an accurate picture, we must have clarity, focus, and the ability to calmly envision the final result. We cannot do this well on our own, especially in times of struggle, when our vision is blurry, fractured, and chaotic. We must trust God's wisdom over our own understanding.

Training Questions:
What does your current path look like?

Are you on the right path? Will this path likely lead where you need to go?

Are you ready to turn around?

Prayer: Gracious God, we thank you for your guidance in showing us a clear and straight path. Give us the courage to follow your directions and stay on the path you provide. In Christ, Amen.

Day Two:

Scripture: John 16:13
However, when the Spirit of Truth comes, he will guide you in all truth. He won't speak on his own, but will say whatever he hears and will proclaim to you what is to come.

Training Principle: God has sent the Holy Spirit to provide wisdom and guidance in your life. The Holy Spirit is your conduit to the Father's plan for you! To see a picture of God's plan, you must listen to the Holy Spirit. Sit quietly now.

Training Questions:
Are you listening?

What is the Spirit saying to you today, through Scripture, friends, and prayer?

Prayer: Gracious God, help me listen to the guidance of the Holy Spirit today, in whatever ways he speaks to me. Give me patience to hear and strength to respond. I pray in the name of Christ, Amen.

Day Three:

Scripture: Jeremiah 29:11
I know the plans I have in mind for you, declares the LORD; they are plans for peace, not disaster, to give you a future filled with hope.

Training Principle: Even in the midst of great confusion, God has a plan for your life. That plan will bring you hope and courage, not despair. In moments of doubt, remind yourself to take a deep breath and trust, so that you can follow where God's plan leads.

Training Questions:
Are you living out God's plan for your life today even in the midst of confusion? What do you see when you imagine your future?

What bright spot of hope, even a small one, can you focus on today?

Prayer: Gracious God, thank you for watching beyond the horizon of where I can see and for your willingness to make the journey with me. In Christ, Amen.

Day Four:

Scripture: James 1:5
But anyone who needs wisdom should ask God, whose very nature is to give to everyone without a second thought, without keeping score. Wisdom will certainly be given to those who ask.

Training Principle: God has a generous plan for your life. However, you must want it—God does not generally force us to accept his plans. Likewise, God willingly offers wisdom and guidance when we ask for help. But many of us never take the time to ask.

Training Questions:
Are you asking for God's guidance and wisdom through your prayers, study, and devotional life today?

If not, where do you go to seek guidance and wisdom?

Do you really want what God has for you? Have you expressed this to God?

Prayer: Gracious God, you are more ready to offer your guidance than I am to ask. Give me the knowledge for where you would have me go and the tenacity to only follow you. In Christ, Amen.

Day Five:

Scripture: Psalm 25:12
Where are the ones who honor the LORD?
  God will teach them which path to take.

Training Principle: To follow God requires deliberately choosing the path God has paved for our lives. God will show you that path and give you the strength to follow it. Fearing God means respecting, avoiding, and clearing the obstacles to that path.

Training Question:
What is blocking your path?

Prayer: Gracious God, help me to clear the debris from the path you have laid out for me, and to choose the way that you have chosen. In Christ, Amen.

Day Six:

Scripture: John 14:16
I will ask the Father, and he will send another Companion, who will be with you forever.

Training Principle: Jesus requests the Holy Spirit to be present in our lives to be our Advocate. The canvas of our life unveils the work of the Holy Spirit.

Training Questions:
What does it mean to have God as your advocate?

How are you called to be an advocate for God in this world?

What are some ways you witness to God's work in your life?

Prayer: Gracious God, thank you for being my best advocate. Give me the courage to be an advocate for your good news and for grace in the world. In Christ, Amen.

Day Seven:

Scripture: Proverbs 2:6-9

The Lord gives wisdom;
from his mouth come knowledge and understanding.
He reserves ability for those with integrity.
He is a shield for those who live a blameless life.
He protects the paths of justice
and guards the way of those who are loyal to him.
Then you will understand righteousness and justice,
as well as integrity, every good course.

Training Principle: God grants not only wisdom and understanding to those who ask but also common sense. As you finalize your picture of victory over your giants, ask God to provide an honest and accurate appraisal of your situation. You are called to love God and to live like God. That requires integrity and faithfulness.

Training Question:
What stands in your way of living like God intends?

Prayer: Gracious God, help me to learn your truths but also to employ them in practical ways in my life. Help me to paint the best picture of your grace within my own life first. I pray in Christ, Amen.

SHARPEN YOUR TOOLS

Discover: This week, discover your spiritual gifts. This may be a completely new idea for you, or you may already be well aware of your gifts. In either case, this is an opportunity for self-assessment. There are several good resources available for gift discovery, including a simple online self-evaluation. You can find it at this link: www.ministrymatters.com/spiritualgifts.

Set aside thirty minutes early this week to do the online gifts assessment, or consult another gifts assessment resource. Write down the key things you learn.

Deepen: As you go through each day, stay alert to your own gifts. Look for the ways your gifts show up naturally in your everyday life. Once you've discovered your gifts, practice being aware of them, and see what you learn about yourself.

Day One:

Scripture: 1 Peter 4:10
And serve each other according to the gift each person has received, as good managers of God's diverse gifts.

Training Principle: You have been given spiritual gifts, and those gifts should be used to serve others.

Training Questions:
What is your spiritual gift(s)?

How do you use it to serve others?

Prayer: Gracious God, thank you for the spiritual gift you have given me. Give me the courage to use it to make a difference to others. I pray in Christ, Amen.

Day Two:

Scripture: 1 Corinthians 12:27-31

You are the body of Christ and parts of each other. In the church, God has appointed first apostles, second prophets, third teachers, then miracles, then gifts of healing, the ability to help others, leadership skills, different kinds of tongues. All aren't apostles, are they? All aren't prophets, are they? All aren't teachers, are they? All don't perform miracles, do they? All don't have gifts of healing, do they? All don't speak in different tongues, do they? All don't interpret, do they? Use your ambition to try to get the greater gifts. And I'm going to show you an even better way.

Training Principle: There are countless spiritual gifts. Each gift has a special function, but as we learn in the Bible, all gifts work for the good of one Body of Christ.

Training Question:

How do your spiritual gifts fit within the overall work of God in the world?

Prayer: Gracious God, help me to not only understand my own spiritual gift but also to use it. Give me a clear picture for how my gift fits within your plan. I pray in Christ, Amen.

Day Three:

Scripture: Romans 12:6-8

We have different gifts that are consistent with God's grace that has been given to us. If your gift is prophecy, you should prophesy in proportion to your faith. If your gift is service, devote yourself to serving. If your gift is teaching, devote yourself to teaching. If your gift is encouragement, devote yourself to encouraging. The one giving should do it with no strings attached. The leader should lead with passion. The one showing mercy should be cheerful.

Training Principle: God has given you a spiritual gift and intends for you to use that gift to the best of your abilities.

Training Questions:

What are you doing to further develop your gift?

How might you do more to deepen and broaden your gift?

Prayer: Gracious God, help me to use my spiritual gifts to do your will in excellent ways. Help me to settle for nothing less than my very best. In Christ I pray, Amen.

Day Four:

Scripture: 1 Corinthians 12:7-11
A demonstration of the Spirit is given to each person for the common good. A word of wisdom is given by the Spirit to one person, a word of knowledge to another according to the same Spirit, faith to still another by the same Spirit, gifts of healing to another in the one Spirit, performance of miracles to another, prophecy to another, the ability to tell spirits apart to another, different kinds of tongues to another, and the interpretation of the tongues to another. All these things are produced by the one and same Spirit who gives what he wants to each person.

Training Principle: The Holy Spirit is the source of our spiritual gifts. Though we have different spiritual gifts, the purpose of each is the same—to help each other and serve God's will on earth. When our gifts are deployed, we experience acts of exceptional faith, healing, and the ability to understand God's will. This is most powerful in the context of a group, where many people are using their gifts, all working together.

Training Questions:
What is God's purpose for your spiritual gift?

How will it help the whole Body of Christ?

Prayer: Gracious God, help me to use my specific spiritual gift with passion and commitment. I want to make a difference in the world and transform the way others see you. In Christ I pray, Amen.

Day Five:

Scripture: Romans 14:5
One person considers some days to be more sacred than others, while another person considers all days to be the same. Each person must have their own convictions.

Training Principle: Every day is an opportunity to make a difference in the world, so sharpening the tools that God has given us must be a daily event.

Training Question:
What have you done today to sharpen the tools that God has given to you?

Prayer: Gracious God, remind me that each day is an opportunity to use the gifts you have given me. Some days are more difficult than others, but I will stay focused on you. In Christ I pray, Amen.

Day Six:

Scripture: 1 Corinthians 13:8
Love never fails. As for prophecies, they will be brought to an end. As for tongues, they will stop. As for knowledge, it will be brought to an end.

Training Principle: The one gift that transcends all is love. Throughout Scripture, we are called to love one another as God has loved us, to see one another as God sees us. Sharpening the tools that God has given us helps us see each other through the eyes of Jesus.

Training Questions:
List the characteristics that exemplify the love of Christ in action.

Do you express the love of Christ in what you do?

Does love permeate your daily routine?

Prayer: Gracious God, I want to love like you love me. Give me the courage to love like Jesus and to set the example for how we should treat each other. In Christ, Amen.

Day Seven:

Scripture: Ephesians 2:8-9
You are saved by God's grace because of your faith. This salvation is God's gift. It's not something you possessed. It's not something you did that you can be proud of.

Training Principle: The most significant weapon for facing the giants of our lives is the gift of salvation offered to us by Christ. The helmet of salvation (Eph. 6) protects our thoughts and aligns our attitudes with God. Facing difficult battles can wear us down. But our salvation in Christ ensures that no matter the battle's result, Christ has won the war. Fight the giants of your life with confidence and strength. Thank God for the gift of salvation.

Prayer: Gracious God, we are blessed by the work of your Son, Jesus, in our lives. Thank you for the gift of salvation. Give us the presence of mind to share our faith and "exercise our faith." In Christ, Amen.

The Third Stone:
DEVELOP A PLAN

Discover: You will need a notebook or pad of paper and a pen or pencil this week. Set aside fifteen minutes each day this week to review the chapter on the Third Stone. Each day, review a portion of the chapter. What questions or ideas does it raise for you, related to strategic planning in your current situation? Jot down all of your questions and ideas. They do not need to be neat or orderly. Just record what comes to mind as you skim the chapter.

Deepen: As you go through your week, mentally begin to construct the framework for your strategic plan. Let the questions and ideas you're discovering lead you. What gaps are appearing in your plan? Where do you need to do more research? What seemed to be important before but seems less important now? As your framework develops, diagram it in your notebook, in a way that makes sense to you.

Day One:

Scripture: James 4:13-15

Pay attention, you who say, "Today or tomorrow we will go to such-and-such a town. We will stay there a year, buying and selling, and making a profit." You don't really know about tomorrow. What is your life? You are a mist that appears for only a short while before it vanishes. Here's what you ought to say: "If the Lord wills, we will live and do this or that."

Training Principle: Life is uncertain. But when we put our trust in God, we establish a firm strategy for tomorrow.

Training Questions:

What is your strategy for confronting the giants in your life?

What do you need to give over to God?

Prayer: Gracious God, so often I scurry through life looking for the easy answers. But I know that much of life is far from easy. Help me to trust you first and allow your wisdom to build the strategy for my next steps. In Christ, Amen.

Day Two:

Scripture: Proverbs 15:22
Plans fail with no counsel,
but with many counselors they succeed.

Training Principle: Scripture tells us that we are created for relationships. Just like the relationship of the Holy Trinity—Father, Son, and Holy Spirit—we need one another for fellowship, strength, and guidance.

Training Questions:
Make a list of those mentors and wise friends in your life whom you turn to for guidance.

Have you consulted them lately?

How might these mentors provide counsel and encouragement for you during your current battle?

Prayer: Gracious God, thank you for the godly friends and mentors that you send to me to provide wisdom and guidance. Help me not to take them for granted and to seek their counsel. In Christ, Amen.

Day Three:

Scripture: Romans 12:1-2

So, brothers and sisters, because of God's mercies, I encourage you to present your bodies as a living sacrifice that is holy and pleasing to God. This is your appropriate priestly service. Don't be conformed to the patterns of this world, but be transformed by the renewing of your minds so that you can figure out what God's will is—what is good and pleasing and mature.

Training Principle: We must offer a willing spirit, in order to develop a solid strategy for confronting the giants of our lives. The Apostle Paul instructs us to give over our hearts and lives to God so that we may understand God's plans for us. He calls this our "sacrifice," and it begins when we make ourselves wholly available to hear and follow God's word and guidance. Our lives will not move in one direction (strategy) while our desires point us in an opposite direction. You must commit to your strategy.

Training Question:

Do your heart and life truly align with God's way? Or are you harboring hesitation, clinging to your own will and desires?

Prayer: Gracious God, I pray that you would give me a willing spirit to follow the strategy that you establish in my life. In Christ, Amen.

Day Four:

Scripture: Luke 14:28-32
"If one of you wanted to build a tower, wouldn't you first sit down and calculate the cost, to determine whether you have enough money to complete it? Otherwise, when you have laid the foundation but couldn't finish the tower, all who see it will begin to belittle you. They will say, 'Here's the person who began construction and couldn't complete it!' Or what king would go to war against another king without first sitting down to consider whether his ten thousand soldiers could go up against the twenty thousand coming against him? And if he didn't think he could win, he would send a representative to discuss terms of peace while his enemy was still a long way off."

Training Principle: When we set out to accomplish something, we must carefully calculate the costs. Jesus used an example of home construction to illustrate the importance of this principle. As we develop a giant-fighting strategy, we must be clear about what it will cost so that we understand the commitment we are making.

Training Questions:
What are the costs for confronting the giants of your life?

Are you willing to incur them?

Prayer: Gracious God, I pray for patience and guidance as I count the cost of confronting the giants in my life. Give me the strength I need to clearly see the costs and the faith to commit to this journey. In Christ, Amen.

Day Five:

Scripture: Isaiah 25:1
LORD, you are my God.
I will exalt you; I will praise your name,
  for you have done wonderful things,
    planned long ago, faithful and sure.

Training Principle: The prophet Isaiah describes God as a planner. He praises God for all of God's wonderful ways and describes God's actions as having been planned from the beginning of time. Gratitude is a critical characteristic of the Christian life, as it helps to keep our hearts turned toward God, and helps us to retain a hopeful, positive outlook.

Training Questions:
Where do you see the wonderful hand of God-the-Divine-Planner in your life and in the world?

Have you expressed your gratitude to God today?

Prayer: Gracious God, I praise you and thank you for your awesome examples of planning in the world. Give me the patience and courage to follow your model. In Christ, Amen.

Day Six:

Scripture: 2 Kings 19:25
Haven't you heard?
I set this up long ago;
   I planned it in the distant past!
Now I have made it happen,
   making fortified cities
      collapse into piles of rubble.

Training Principle: God is to be praised for his marvelous work. God is also to be trusted, for God's careful planning delivers results. "Now I have made it happen," God says. God-led plans can yield results that are greater than we could ever imagine or plan on our own. Be confident that your God-led plan will result in good things.

Training Questions:
Have you experienced a time when things turned out all right— or even better than all right, after a period of struggle, when you had little hope for any positive outcome?

What would happen if you were given absolute proof that your careful planning would lead to good things? How might you feel and behave differently?

Prayer: Gracious God, thank you for providing all the proof I need to trust in the goodness of your plans. Help me to know that, even if I cannot see the outcome, you are there to aid and guide me to the fruition of my God-led plans. In Christ, Amen.

Day Seven:

Scripture: Proverbs 19:21
*Many plans are in a person's mind,
but the LORD's purpose will succeed.*

Training Principle: Do your plans match God's? Your plan must align with God's plan. Proverbs teaches us that our efforts are useless when our plan diverts us from God's will. As followers of Christ we align our plans with God's through daily prayer and by focusing our thoughts and actions—training to be more Christ-like. That's what you are doing now—so be encouraged and keep it up!

Prayer: Gracious God, I thank you for caring enough about me—about all of us—that you have developed a plan for our lives. Help me to follow your plan and make your will a priority in my life. In Christ, Amen.

TRAIN FOR VICTORY

Discovery: Successful exercise and weight loss programs often require participants to log their food and caloric intake, and the details of their workouts, including weight and number of reps. The simple act of recording something in writing seems to motivate people to stay on track. You will use your notebook or pad of paper again this week to do the same thing. At the end of each day this week, spend a few minutes logging your spiritual routine from the day. Did you pray? If so, when and what effect did it have on you? Did you sense God's presence in some way that day? If so, describe it. Did you find a way to serve another person? Write a few words about it. Use this log-in time to assess the day from a spiritual perspective, to see where you are gaining strength and where you still need work. This spiritual journaling can be a form of training itself.

Deepen: Be mindful of your spiritual life each day this week. Stay alert to the presence of Christ, and when you feel yourself stepping away from that presence, stop, refocus, and return.

Day One:

Scripture: 2 Timothy 1:7
God didn't give us a spirit that is timid but one that is powerful, loving, and self-controlled.

Training Principle: We must use self-discipline in order to understand and live out God's plans in our lives. We must engage in a routine of prayer, devotion, service, and fellowship.

Training Questions:
How would you describe the spiritual routines in your life?

Do they lead you closer to God?

Prayer: Gracious God, give me a state of mind to seek after spiritual discipline in my life. Help me to serve you by first growing deeper and more faithful in your Word. I pray in Christ, Amen.

Day Two:

Scripture: 1 Timothy 4:7-8
Train yourself for a holy life! While physical training has some value, train-ing in holy living is useful for everything. It has promise for this life now and the life to come.

Training Principle: A successful training regimen requires com-mitment. Consistent training develops our strength and capac-ity to serve God. Paul encourages Timothy that just as physical training provides great benefits for the body, spiritual training provides even more significant benefits for our growth.

Training Questions:
Do you follow a physical training regimen? How does this im-pact your body?

How might a spiritual training regimen impact your faith, your spiritual strength?

Prayer: Gracious God, thank you for the bodies you gave us, and for encouraging us to keep them strong and healthy. Help me to remember that you expect even more for our spiritual health. Give me the strength and focus I need to stay committed to the spiritually disciplined life. In Christ, Amen.

Day Three:

Scripture: Proverbs 10:17
Those who heed instruction
  are on the way to life,
  but those who ignore correction
  lose their way.

Training Principle: A life of discipline leads to a life of service and purpose in God. This same discipline builds strength for battles with the giants of our life.

Training Question:
How would you assess your level of spiritual discipline today?

Prayer: Gracious God, I pray for strength to stay at the task of growing deeper in your love and serving faithfully in your grace. Give me the wisdom to stay at the task of becoming more like you. In Christ, Amen.

Day Four:

Scripture: Hebrews 12:11
No discipline is fun while it lasts, but it seems painful at the time. Later, however, it yields the peaceful fruit of righteousness for those who have been trained by it.

Training Principle: Effective exercise requires hard work. Working day in and day out to build a healthy body takes commitment and tenacity. The same is required to build a healthy spirit. The rewards are clear—spiritual discipline strengthens our relationship with God and each other, and provides a clear path for facing the world.

Training Question:
What is one reward of the spiritually disciplined life that you especially long for? Focus on that reward today, and allow this to motivate you to stay committed.

Prayer: Gracious God, thank you for your commitment to your people and for the ways you call us to a disciplined, faithful life. Remind me of the rewards of this life, God, and use them to help me stay on track. Thank you for your presence in this journey. In Christ, Amen.

Day Five:

Scripture: Luke 6:40
Disciples aren't greater than their teacher, but whoever is fully prepared will be like their teacher.

Training Principle: The more we work and train, the more proficient we become in our skills and the use of our gifts. Our training is meant not only to strengthen us but to aid others. As we use our gifts, we become examples, teachers, and models for the people around us.

Training Questions:
Think of all the people you encounter each week, from family to strangers you meet in daily life.

In what ways might your training be a positive example for others?

How might your ever-stronger gifts be useful and encouraging for others?

Prayer: Gracious God, thank you for the example we have in Christ. Help me to use my training and my gifts to serve others, as Jesus did, even when I am in the difficult valleys of life. Show me how to be a positive influence, and remind me daily to keep my eyes on you, dear God. I pray in the name of Christ, Amen.

Day Six:

Scripture: James 1:12
Those who stand firm during testing are blessed. They are tried and true. They will receive the life God has promised to those who love him as their reward.

Training Principle: One of the most challenging parts of any training regimen is simply staying on course. Not giving up. Not giving in to discouragement. Not throwing in the towel when we are weary. In training, as in all of life, we must focus on the promises and faithfulness of God. Remember that God wants only good for us and, through the presence of the Holy Spirit, God gives us the strength and hope we need when we feel like giving up. If you are struggling to stand firm, ask God to renew you, to help you stay on course.

Training Questions:
How would you describe the current status of your spiritual training?

Are you standing firm, motivated, sticking to your routine and optimistic about what lies ahead for you?

If not, what is getting in your way, and what are you doing to get back on course? Start by asking for God's help.

Prayer: Gracious God, I thank you for your presence in my life. When I am discouraged, please lift me up so that I can stand firm. Help me to hear your voice of encouragement when I feel like giving up, and help me to turn away from distractions and detours that might lure me off course. Remind me that following you is always the right thing, even when I am weary. Amen.

Day Seven:

Scripture: 1 Corinthians 9:25-27

Everyone who competes practices self-discipline in everything. The runners do this to get a crown of leaves that shrivel up and die, but we do it to receive a crown that never dies. So now this is how I run—not without a clear goal in sight. I fight like a boxer in the ring, not like someone who is shadowboxing. Rather, I'm landing punches on my own body and subduing it like a slave. I do this to be sure that I myself won't be disqualified after preaching to others.

Training Principle: Why do elite athletes work so hard? Because they train not only to win a contest but to become the best they can possibly be. They train intensely again and again. And so we must train for Christ. As Paul states, "we train like an athlete" not for an earthly prize but for one that is eternal. Pause to think about and appreciate the eternal value of your hard work and tenacity.

Prayer: Gracious God, thank you for the opportunity to work hard, for the eternal prize you offer. Thank you for giving me a tenacious spirit! Remind me that I do have it, for I so often forget and give in to self-doubt. Give me enthusiasm to keep moving forward and the assurance that all I do for you is useful. In Christ, Amen.

RUN BOLDLY TO MEET THE GIANT

Discover: Use this week to review your progress from the last four weeks. Acknowledge how far you have come and the ways you have already grown. Recognize the ways you are now more prepared to meet the giants of life. Look back over your picture, the assessment of your spiritual gifts, your strategic plan, and your spiritual training log. Would it benefit you to spend more time with one of these? If so, do it this week. This is your time to finish your visioning, preparation, planning, and training. You have all you need in order to meet the giant.

Deepen: What is your next step?

Day One:

Scripture: Ephesians 3:12
In Christ we have bold and confident access to God through faith in him.

Training Principle: The work of Christ gives us a new place close to the heart of God. Because of Christ in our lives, we can confront our struggles in this world with boldness. Like the shepherd boy David, we are big enough.

Training Question:
In what part of your life do you most need courage to be bold?

Prayer: Gracious God, thank you for your presence in my life, and for the strength and security it provides. Thank you for showing me that I can live boldly. Give me courage to be the person you have created me to be. In Christ, Amen.

Day Two:

Scripture: Hebrews 10:19
Brothers and sisters, we have confidence that we can enter the holy of holies by means of Jesus' blood.

Training Principle: The work of Christ in our lives gives us access to God's holiest place—his heart. What a powerful place to be. We are God's family.

Training Questions:
What is the holiest place you can imagine? Is it a place of worship—a cathedral, country church, or chapel? Is it the place where you met God for the first time or where God called you to something new? Imagine yourself dwelling there now, with God.

Prayer: Gracious God, thank you for making us family and for welcoming us into your heart. Help me never to take that gift for granted. In Christ, Amen.

Day Three:

Scripture: 1 Timothy 3:13
Those who have served well gain a good standing and considerable confidence in the faith that is in Christ Jesus.

Training Principle: During Paul's time, the first stage of leadership was a deacon. The deacon was the "servant" of the Church, providing oversight for the various ways God unveils God's love for humanity. Paul reminded Timothy that those who work faithfully in service to God gain confidence to serve boldly. And, the more boldly they serve, the more confidence they gain.

Training Questions:
Look back at the ways you have served God, the church, and other people.

How have even the "small" acts of service helped you to grow and to gain confidence?

What are you able to do with confidence today, but would have lacked the confidence to do before?

Prayer: Gracious God, thank you for giving me the gift of faith and the opportunity to put it into action. Help me to not shrink back from the opportunities you place before me. In Christ, Amen.

Day Four:

Scripture: Matthew 7:7
"Ask, and you will receive. Search, and you will find. Knock, and the door will be opened to you."

Training Principle: The image of a child persistently asking for a new toy or a piece of candy strikes a chord with most of us—because we have been that child. Our relationship with God should be dynamic and real like the best type of parent-child relationship. So be persistent when you ask for God's mercy and blessing. Keep asking, and do so boldly. Pray boldly and with great confidence.

Training Questions:
Is there something you need, but are hesitant to ask for from God?

What do you think is at the root of your hesitation?

Can you let go of that hesitation and pray openly and boldly for what you need? Try it.

Prayer: Gracious God, we thank you for teaching us to ask boldly for your presence and your will. In Christ, Amen.

Day Five:

Scripture: Deuteronomy 31:6
Be strong! Be fearless! Don't be afraid and don't be scared by your enemies, because the LORD your God is the one who marches with you. He won't let you down, and he won't abandon you.

Training Principle: God promises to go before us and to keep us from falling. You will not be discarded. God will give you courage for your battles. God claims you as God's.

Training Questions:
List the decisions you must make.

As you continue to move forward, making decisions and taking action, what might help you to claim God's presence with you? Could you memorize all or part of the above verse from Deuteronomy?

Prayer: Gracious God, grant me the courage to face my giants. I claim the promise that you go before me, and that you stay with me. Help me to go forward with boldness. In Christ, Amen.

Day Six:

Scripture: 1 Corinthians 16:13
Stay awake, stand firm in your faith, be brave, be strong.

Training Principle: Be on guard. Stand firm. Be courageous. Be strong. Giants do not like courageous people. So discard your fear and claim your gifts. Show your faith boldly, while your giant bares his slobbery teeth. Recognize your own strength.

Training Questions:
What image can you use to focus yourself, when you need to stay awake, stand firm, be brave, and be strong?

Is there a photo or other image that you can keep in mind as you continue marching forward?

Prayer: Gracious God, I pray for courage and for strength to become all that you have in store for me. Help me to be on guard and to remember what strength looks like. In Christ, Amen.

Day Seven:

Scripture: Proverbs 28:1
The wicked run away even though no one pursues them,
but the righteous are as confident as a lion.

Training Principle: David was young, inexperienced, and alone. But he was also bold. He trusted his faith in God and thus became a giant killer. You are a giant killer. The giants have no hold over you. Don't give up. Keep moving forward. As Scripture states, not only will you defeat lions, you will become as bold as one.

Prayer: Gracious God, help me to take hold of the promises you have made for me. I am not defeated. You are with me, and I have victory in you. In Christ, Amen.

SURRENDER:
WHEN WE BECOME
OUR OWN GIANT

BY SHANE STANFORD

It may seem strange to include a chapter entitled "Surrender" in a book about conquering your giants. The previous discussions in *Five Stones* reminded each of us that we were created to be giant killers and God has gifted each of us with the appropriate tools to win the battle against our toughest struggles.

However, if we read further in to the journey of David in Scripture, we realize that the story does not stop at his encounter with Goliath. David faces more giants after his fight with the Philistine warrior, including a struggle with King Saul, a host of foreign kings and invaders, and members of his own court and family. David's life after Goliath becomes the stuff of legend, and, yes, he does become king. He also transforms his legacy into a witness for his faith. No one in Scripture but David has been referred to as a "man after God's own heart." David's life is marked by his deep love for God and by his desire to live for God the rest of his days.

God was equally smitten with David. David's faithful life engaged the love and favor of God as seen on this planet in only one other experience, that of the birth of God's son, Jesus. God's favor for David was so great that it prompted God to exclaim in 2 Samuel 7, "I will make your name as famous as anyone who has ever lived on the earth!" It doesn't get any better than that. Oh, how we wish the story ended there.

But it doesn't. David must wage the greatest battle of his life against the least expected giant: himself. You need only to read 2 Samuel 11 and subsequent chapters in order to learn of David's dramatic fall. In those chapters, David's life takes a major turn while simply walking on the roof of his palace one night. It is then that he sees a young woman bathing on the roof of her own home some distance away. Her name was Bathsheba. There on the rooftop David encountered a giant he had not expected, and one that made Goliath look like a playful kitten. David met the giant of himself.

Psalm 51 may best express what it feels like to confront the giant of one's own arrogance and hubris. Thus far in *Five Stones* we have equipped you to face external giants. Now we turn to the giants within.

One Spark

Read 2 Samuel 11 and 12 and Psalm 51

The unfolding tragedy of David and Bathsheba reminds me of the story of Jack Reston. Jack was a mill worker who lived in the city of Boston at the end of the nineteenth century. Jack had a family—a beautiful wife, and a son and daughter. One night in May of 1894, Jack arrived home from work to find his house, along with most of his street and neighborhood, engulfed by a raging fire. By the end of the evening, total loss would face this man who faithfully got up every morning, went off to the mill, and worked eighteen to twenty hours just to put food on the table, providing the best that he could. Of course, all of this took place long before there were federal assistance programs. People mostly fended for themselves, and it was all the more important for people to watch out for each other.

Jack would learn later that his home had caught fire from the house to his right, which had caught fire from the row of succeeding homes on the street where they lived. The simple wood frames burned easily, spreading the carnage from house to house. The burning took place in quick order, too quickly for anything to be done or for much to be saved.

The first house in the neighborhood to burn was ignited from the factory warehouse in the back of their neighborhood. Most Boston neighborhoods in those days sat closely to industrial corridors. Industrial and housing areas were in close proximity so that people could walk to work with ease. The warehouse was of flammable materials that were ready for shipment, and it was no surprise that once they caught fire, things moved rapidly from there. The warehouse ignited from the embers of an apartment complex just a few hundred yards across the block.

The apartments caught fire and set ablaze as a result of the depot that was built next to them just a couple of years before. The depot, which was one of the most beautiful and useful buildings in the city, caught fire from the city baseball park, where the Boston Bean Eaters played.

And, the city baseball park, which sat at the end of Walpall Street and was one of the grandest stadiums in all of baseball at that time, in the late 1800s, ignited because a fan dropped his lit cigarette in between the bleachers and it landed in barrels of trash. The cigarette fell from the fan's hand after he had been shoved when a brawl broke out between the players and fans of the Boston Bean Eaters and the Baltimore Orioles.

The fight broke out because a soon-to-be-great player for the Orioles named John McGraw got into a fistfight with the third baseman from the Bean Eaters. So from that one moment—from the brawl, to the dropped cigarette, to the fire that burned 107 buildings and homes to the ground, a man named Jack Reston ultimately lost all that was dear to him.

One bad decision has the potential to change the world, even a decision that seems insignificant at the time. One moment of weakness can change lives. We must work to understand the places where we are the most vulnerable, the places where a spark could change everything. The worst fires are often lit as a result of weaknesses and bad decisions.

The giants of pride, arrogance, and guilt work hand in hand. They are cousins to the emotions and destructive habits that lead to bad decisions and terrible outcomes in our lives. The first two—pride and arrogance—can appear harmless enough until they cause us to make that one comment or action that sends the dominoes falling. Eventually we realize, sometimes early, but mostly too late, that far too many dominoes have fallen to keep the mess a secret. And so we find ourselves racing to either repair the breach or to hide the damage.

I have mentioned many times in my ministry that I don't believe anyone gets up in the morning and says, "Today, I believe I will destroy my life." But I know countless individuals who make one very bad decision, which leads to ten more bad decisions, and on and on it goes. It is possible to wake up eventually and ask, "How did I make this mess?" But by then, the damage may be irreparable.

That was David's story with Bathsheba, and I am afraid it is far too often the story for most of us, as well.

We wake up, recognizing the mess we have made, and then we feel guilty. Guilt is even more dangerous than pride or arrogance, because guilt does not let go easily, even after pride and arrogance are put into their place. One theologian says that guilt is the most dangerous of our ill-fated expressions because guilt comes in three forms:

The guilt that defines our past: I will never be forgiven for what I have done.

The guilt that defines our present: I don't like who I am, because what I am doing is wrong.

The guilt that defines our future: I will always do wrong. I will never be able to change.

Any one of these three can dominate our thinking and our lives, at any time. Guilt becomes the voice that tells us what to believe about ourselves. Guilt is insidious and persistent. Guilt can seem inescapable.

Consider the man who never could please his mother, because in her estimation he never called home often enough. He could not escape the long reach of guilt, no matter what he did. Their conversation went something like this:

The man called his mother in Florida. "Mom, how are you?"

"Not too good," says the mother. "I've been very weak."

The son says, "Why are you so weak? Are you sick?"

She says, "Because I haven't eaten in thirty-eight days."

The man says, "That's terrible. Why haven't you eaten in thirty-eight days?"

The mother answers, "Because I didn't want my mouth to be filled with food if you should call."

Most guilt is unproductive and becomes a weighty burden that we can never bear. Sometimes, however, guilt is valuable and speaks truth to us when others can't get through. This was the case with David. His guilt dominated and defined his life, but he refused to listen to it until the prophet Nathan forced him to face this all-too-powerful giant. Read the interchange yourself, in 2 Samuel 12, to hear the dialogue between the king and the prophet. The most important phrase you will read is Nathan's words to David: "You are that man."

Honestly, too many times, I am that man too, and I would suppose you can be as well.

How do we face the giants borne of our own weakness?

David's story teaches us three lessons on this topic.

Confession

A pastor friend likes to say that "Penitence is the other side of arrogance, and confession is the other side of pride." How true. David's guilt wrapped him up so that he could only see his life from one angle. His pride and arrogance kept him from seeing the whole picture of his life. When the giant lives inside of you, drawing a clear picture means opening up the places deep inside your own soul and having the courage to look in. That is not easy, especially when you are used to making decisions like a king.

David's confession to Nathan drove David to his knees and forced him to see the whole picture of his sin and brokenness. His giants of pride and arrogance had nowhere to run. The lights were turned on and the truth, though painful in the moment, was healing the wound as it was exposed to the light. David had to experience this painful time in order to grow beyond his broken nature.

I love the story of the emperor moth. The cocoon of the emperor moth is flask-like in shape. To develop into a perfect insect, the moth must force its way through the neck of the cocoon by hours of intense struggle. Entomologists explain that this pressure to which the moth is subjected is nature's way of forcing a life-giving substance into the moth's wings.

There is a story about a man who happened upon an emperor moth cocoon one day. Curious, he took the cocoon home for observation. Soon he noticed the moth struggling to break free, in seemingly needless pain. Wanting to help, the man took a small pair of scissors and snipped the restraining threads, making the moth's emergence painless and effortless. The creature never developed wings. During the brief time before its death, it could only crawl weakly along a surface and was never able to fly through the air with its rainbow-colored wings. Sorrow, suffering, trials, and tribulations grow us into Christlikeness. The refining and developing processes are often slow and sometimes painful. But through grace we emerge triumphant. With his confession, David began the process of becoming new again.

Discovering "Original Grace"

We have all heard about original sin—the belief that humanity is born sinful and broken. I believe that we are born with the image of God distorted, but I also believe we have enough of that original image to be reminded from where we come and to whom we belong. The real struggle happens because, like David, our pride and arrogance begin to define the journey more than our relationship with God does.

That is why the concept of "original grace" is so important, especially in dealing with guilt. Guilt strikes at our core by convincing us that we have lost not only our way but also our value. Original grace, as I like to call it, reminds us that God has gone to great lengths to bring us into relationship and set things right with us; therefore, we will not fall from God's care so easily, no matter our transgression.

This is a tough lesson for David to experience, especially in front of the prophet Nathan. Original grace directly contradicts our pride and sense of self-sufficiency. It ultimately points the whole of us—warts and all—back to God and reminds us that God sees everything about us—good and bad.

David could not find restoration and freedom from his giant of guilt until he understood that his best tool for fighting that giant began with his humility rather than his abilities. David recognized that he had received forgiveness from the God he had wronged. In that recognition, David realized that he, himself, was the greatest stumbling block to his own healing. There was nothing David could say or do to make right his transgressions. His only hope was found in God.

Kings tend to make grand "I am" statements. "I am pleased. I am displeased. I am ruler of the kingdom." It must be utterly humiliating for a king to face his own failure: "I am the reason for my own downfall."

Original grace replaces the hubris of our "I am" statements with a new and better set of statements. The Scriptures tell of Jesus saying "I am" seven particular times. These are known as the I AM statements of Jesus.

1. The Bread of Life

Then Jesus declared, "I am the bread of life. He who comes to me will never go hungry, and he who believes in me will never be thirsty. (John 6:35 NIV)

2. The Light of the World

When Jesus spoke again to the people, he said, "I am the light of the world. Whoever follows me will never walk in darkness, but will have the light of life." (John 8:12 NIV)

3. The Gate

I am the gate; whoever enters through me will be saved. They will come in and go out, and find pasture. (John 10:9 NIV)

4. The Good Shepherd

I am the good shepherd. The good shepherd lays down his life for the sheep. (John 10:11 NIV)

5. The Resurrection and the Life

Jesus said to her, "I am the resurrection and the life. Whoever believes in me will live, even though they die. Everyone who lives and believes in me will never die. Do you believe this?" (John 11:25-26 NIV)

6. The Way, The Truth, And The Life

Jesus answered, "I am the way and the truth and the life. No one comes to the Father except through me." (John 14:6 NIV)

7. The Vine

"I am the vine; you are the branches. If you remain in me and I in you, then you will produce much fruit. Without me, you can't do anything." (John 15:5)

After his confrontation with Nathan, David gave up his illusions. He knew that he was no longer in charge. He gave up his life to God's mercy, love, and grace. Every time I read this section of David's story, I think of John Newton's great hymn, "Amazing Grace."

> *Amazing grace how sweet the sound, that saved a wretch like me.*
>
> *I once was lost, but now am found; was blind, but now I see.*

The lyrics are powerful because Newton wrote the song not about some grand and glorious evangelistic crusade but because of what God had done deep inside of Newton himself—a former slave captain who became freer than he could have ever un-derstood before this "grace appeared."

Surrender

David did exactly what he needed to do in order to sur-vive the confrontation with the giant of himself: he surrendered. I know it may initially sound strange to spend an entire book learning how to fight and win only to be told to surrender. A Japanese spiritual master once told me, "Our greatest battles in life happen within here (pointing to his head and heart), and our greatest tools for victory begin with this (putting his hands into a prayer attention and closing his eyes)." Indeed.

When David had done all he could to stand on his own abil-ity, he stood tallest by collapsing in surrender.

I love the story of family therapist Bruce Larson, who tells how he helped people struggling to surrender their lives to Christ:

> For many years I worked in New York City and coun-seled at my office any number of people who were wrestling with this yes-or-no decision. Often I would suggest they walk with me from my office down to the RCA Building on Fifth Avenue. In the entrance of that building is a gigantic statue of Atlas, a beautifully proportioned man who, with all his muscles strain-ing, is holding the world upon his shoulders. There he is, the most powerfully built man in the world, and he can barely stand up under this burden. "Now that's one way to live," I would point out to my

companion, "trying to carry the world on your shoulders. But now come across the street with me."

On the other side of Fifth Avenue is Saint Patrick's Cathedral, and there behind the high altar is a little shrine of the boy Jesus, perhaps eight or nine years old, and with no effort he is holding the world in one hand. My point was illustrated graphically.

"We have a choice. We can carry the world on our shoulders, or we can say, 'I give up, Lord; here's my life. I give you my world, the whole world.'"

Let me put the point in yet another way, with homage to *Star Wars.* Remember when Obi Wan fought Darth Vader while Luke, Han, and the gang were trying to make it back to the Falcon? When he knew they were safe, Obi Wan simply put down his weapon. Vader struck Obi Wan down. But, we learn later, that Obi Wan's "surrender" made him more powerful than ever. For *Star Wars* fans, perhaps this story helps to make my case.

How do you kill a giant that is, well...you...me...us? We can't win that one. Someone else has to fight the fight for us. Jesus did, and won.

A few years ago, an angry man rushed through the Rijksmuseum in Amsterdam until he reached Rembrandt's famous painting *The Night Watch.* He took out a knife and slashed the masterpiece repeatedly before he could be stopped. A short time later, a distraught, hostile man slipped into St. Peter's Cathedral in Rome with a hammer and began to smash Michelangelo's extraordinary sculpture *Pietà.* These two cherished works of art were severely damaged, some might say destroyed. What did museum officials and curators do? Throw the shredded painting and the shattered sculpture out? Hide them away in a cellar and forget about them? Absolutely not. They called in the best experts who worked with care and precision to restore the treasures.

By His sovereign grace, God can bring good out of our failures, and even out of our sins.

J. Stuart Holden tells of an old Scottish mansion close to where he had his little summer home. One day, a pitcher of soda water was accidentally spilled on a freshly decorated wall, leaving an unsightly stain. The English artist Edwin Henry Landseer happened to be a guest in the house at the time. One day when the family went out to the moors, Landseer stayed behind. With a few masterful strokes of a piece of charcoal, that ugly spot became the outline of a beautiful waterfall, bordered by trees and wildlife. The artist turned the disfigured wall into one of his most successful depictions of Highland life.

You are a giant killer. No giant, no matter where it resides, deserves control over your life. I will say it again. You were created for a purpose, not to suffer destruction at the hands of any giant.

In Psalm 51, David unveils his heart in dramatic fashion when he says to God, "I know that you don't want my wailing and excuses. You want truth."

My own version of David's prayer goes something like this: "God, I recognize that you want the real me. The hurting, angry, unsure, unsettled me. This bare, cracked, splotchy plaster wall is the real deal. And I know you can make something beautiful out of it."

AFTERWORD

by BRAD MARTIN

Shane and I wrote this book to give encouragement and support to those who have faced giants, are facing giants, and will face giants in their lives. In the book, we tell personal stories of the challenges that *we* have faced, and we warn you that giants appear suddenly in life, without notice. In fact, I must share with you that this has happened to Shane. As we were finishing the manuscript of *Five Stones,* Shane received the news that he would face nearly a year of potentially debilitating chemotherapy to treat a dangerous liver disease.

My partner in writing this book never considered surrendering to this giant or running away. Instead, with his doctors armed with their weapons, his co-workers standing tall, his family by his side, and his congregation on its knees, Shane has charged boldly at the giant.

Shane is in the midst of his treatment at this writing, and it is a difficult battle. But he has drawn a clear picture of a return to health, and he is confident, as am I, that he will cut off the head of this killer. Shane is keenly aware of God's presence in his life. And, as he wrote on the preceding page, he knows God will "make something beautiful" out of even this, no matter what happens.

Shane has taught us how to defeat our giants. Now he is showing us how to do so.